Remembering the

FUTURE

THE

NEW

YORK

WORLD'S

FAIR

FROM

1939

TO

1964

Introduction by Robert Rosenblum

Essays by Rosemarie Haag Bletter,
Morris Dickstein, Helen A.
Harrison, Marc H. Miller, Sheldon
J. Reaven, Ileen Sheppard

Remembering the

FUTURE

THE

NEW

YORK

WORLD'S

FAIR

FROM

1939

TO

1964

The Queens Museum

RIZZOLI
NEW YORK

First published in the United States of America in 1989 by
RIZZOLI INTERNATIONAL PUBLICATIONS, INC.
300 Park Avenue South, New York, NY 10010

Copyright © 1989 The Queens Museum

Library of Congress Cataloging-in-Publication Data

Remembering the future : the New York World's Fair from 1939–1964 /
    introduction by Robert Rosenblum : essays by Rosemarie Haag Bletter
    . . . [et al.].
        p.   cm.
    Published in conjunction with a landmark exhibition at the Queens
Museum, New York.
    Bibliography: p. 208
    Includes index.
    ISBN 0-8478-1122-0
    1. New York World's Fair (1964—1965)—History. 2. New York
World's Fair (1939–1940)—History.   I. Bletter, Rosemarie Haag.
II. Queens Museum.
T786 1964.B1R45   1989   89-45432
907.4'747'243—dc20   CIP

This book is published to accompany the exhibition
*Remembering the Future:
The New York World's Fair
from 1939 to 1964.*
The Queens Museum
September 7–December 31, 1989
Exhibition curators: Ileen
Sheppard, Marc H. Miller
Major support for this project has
been provided by *New York
Newsday.* Additional support has
been provided by the New York
State Council on the Arts;
Triborough Bridge & Tunnel
Authority; York Ladder & Scaffold;
David Rockefeller; and the
Electronic Industries Association.

The Queens Museum
New York City Building
Flushing Meadow Park
Flushing, New York 11368

The Queens Museum is housed in
the New York City Building which is
owned by the City of New York, and
its operation is supported in part
with public funds provided by the
New York City Department of
Cultural Affairs, and the Office of
the Queens Borough President,
Claire Shulman. Additional support
is provided with public funds from
the New York State Legislature
and the New York State Council
on the Arts.

Designed by Richelle J. Huff
Set in type by David E. Seham Associates, Metuchen, New Jersey
Printed and bound by Dai Nippon, Tokyo, Japan

CONTENTS

ACKNOWLEDGMENTS

The complex phenomenon known as the World's Fair continues to draw enthusiastic attention from the general public and scholars alike. On the sentimental level, the broad appeal of the Fairs is tied to their potential to bring back vivid memories of times gone by. On the scholarly side, the study of the themes, style, and characteristics of the Fairs reveals much about the spirit and philosophy of their times.

This publication marks the 50th and 25th Anniversaries of the 1939/40 and 1964/65 New York World's Fairs. Like the time capsules buried beneath Flushing Meadow, each of these Fairs presents a revealing portrait of American society. The 1939/40 Fair was promoted optimistically as "the Dawn of a New Day," despite the harsh realities of the Depression years and the ominous threat of World War II. In 1964, the dawn of the space age gave the visions of 1939 a heightened but more qualified consciousness, as expressed by that Fair's awkward theme, "Man in a Shrinking Globe in an Expanding Universe."

A number of the attributes of The Queens Museum have led inevitably to its role as a study center for the two New York World's Fairs. Located in the New York City Building, one of only two structures which remain from the 1939/40 Fair, the Museum lies directly adjacent to the theme center for both Fairs, now occupied by the Unisphere. A permanent exhibit, *The Panorama of the City of New York,* was commissioned by Robert Moses as the centerpiece of the City Building for the 1964/65 Fair. The Museum has built a major collection and archive of World's Fair material and has initiated a variety of scholarly projects concerning the Fairs, notably the 1980 exhibition and publication, *Dawn of a New Day, The New York World's Fair, 1939/40. Remembering the Future* is a natural complement to our previous efforts, exploring in depth the 1964/65 Fair, and drawing on its 1939/40 precursor for contrast and comparison.

The Museum is deeply grateful to Ileen Sheppard, Director of Exhibitions, who served as project director for *Remembering the Future,* and who, in consultation with Marc H. Miller, Curator, selected the exhibition. We are also indebted to our project advisors who provided much guidance during the planning phase of the project and contributed thoughtful and provocative essays: Rosemarie Haag Bletter, Morris Dickstein, Helen A. Harrison, and Sheldon J. Reaven. We also wish to thank Robert Rosenblum for his lively and personal introductory essay.

Members of the Museum staff who have worked closely with Ms. Sheppard include Phyllis Bilick, Anne Edgar, Sonia Kroell, Kathryn Padovano, David Rodriguez, and Louise Weinberg. Special thanks go to research assistants on the project, Peter Balis and Cheryl Epstein Wolf. Additionally, several members of the staff of the Museum of the City of New York have been most helpful in coordinating education and outreach programming for the exhibition. They are: Rick Beard, Maude Coyle, Pam Myers, and Bonnie Yochelson.

The Museum has been pleased to work with Rizzoli International on the publication of this book and particular thanks are given to Robert Janjigian who has been extremely supportive throughout our collaboration. We are also grateful to Richelle J. Huff for the book design and Sara Blackburn for editorial work. Jeffrey Strean also deserves special mention for

Opposite: Night view of the 1964/65 World's Fair. Photography by Bob Golby, collection of The Queens Museum

his outstanding work in the design of the exhibition.

The following individuals, institutions, and corporations have very generously provided objects and photographs for the exhibition and publication: Joseph H. Flad; Portledge School; Bud Gibbs, Executor, Estate of Joe Mielziner; Greenwich Auction House; Pady Blackwood; Ellsworth Kelly; Aileen Gaughan, Walter Dorwin Teague Associates; Sara Roszak; Hugh Wells, General Motors Corporation; The Hagley Museum and Library; Michael and Joy Brown; Janet Parks, Avery Architectural and Fine Arts Library, Columbia University; Jonathan Herman, New York Hall of Science; Tom John; George Jamison, General Electric Corporation; Bill West, NCR Corporation; Joe Bedway, Albert Kahn Associates Inc; Photofind Gallery; Tim Tyson, Marshall Space Flight Center; Thomas C. Howard; Rare Books and Manuscripts Division, New York Public Library; E.I. Du Pont De Nemours & Company; Shelly Lee, Visual Artists Gallery Association; Jim Strong; Clarke + Rapuano; Faith Schornick, Skidmore, Owings & Merrill; Kevin Roche, John Dinkeloo and Associates; The Daily News; UPI/ Bettmann Newsphotos; Elizabeth Gallen, Magnum Photos, Inc; Gordon Lempke, Betsy Richman, Van Romans, Gene Whiskerson, Walt Disney Imagineering; Charles Koulbanis; Costas Machlouzarides; Grace Borgenicht Gallery; Mrs. Mary Ann Serra; Allan D'Arcangelo; Whitney Darrow Jr; United States Information Agency; Childs Gallery; Howard Jean Lipman; Herb Rolfes; Peter Warner; Edward Orth; John Riccardelli; David Oats; Herbert F. Johnson Museum of Art; William P. Suitor; Franklin D. Roosevelt Library; Mr. & Mrs. Jules Kay; Amway Corporation; Marshall Fredericks; John Locke; Charles Ruch, Westinghouse Electric Corporation; Kenneth Snelson; Alfred Stern; Travelers Insurance Company; Photofest; Marilynn Motto; Kimiko and John Powers; Melvyn Kaufman; Arnold P. Chase; Paul Rudolph;

Peter A. Leavens; Laurence Miller Gallery; Fraenkel Gallery; John Bowman; The Phillips Collection; The Queens Borough Public Library; National Geographic Magazine; National Museum of American Art, Smithsonian Institution; Michael Sullivan and Barbara Jones, IBM; Gert Berliner; Edith Luytens Bel Geddes; and Michael and Carolyn Bishop.

In the course of developing this project, many people have provided us with valuable information about the Fairs and clues as to the whereabouts of materials. Our great thanks are given to all who have assisted us and particularly to: Susan Grant Lewin, Adriana Cento, Arnold H. Vollmer, Lady Malcolm Douglas Hamilton, Richard Wills, Frank McCann, Ellen Gartrell, Katherine Kuh, Max Abramovitz, Harold Blake, Joe Ivanick, Charles Schwartz, Laura Rosen, Joan Firestone, Gerard Malanga, Alan Moore, Peter Martecchini, Kevin Boland, Philip Johnson, Ralph Caplan, Gloria Weiner, Marvin Heiferman, Deanne Stillman, Donald R. Sango, Ruth Charney, John Perreault, Jeff Weinstein, Cindy Frye Collins, Patricia Horne, Michael Blake Jr., Larry Paul, and Fiona Irving.

Major support for this project has been provided by New York Newsday. Additional support has been provided by the New York State Council on the Arts, Triborough Bridge & Tunnel Authority, York Ladder & Scaffold, David Rockefeller, and the Electronic Industries Association. We gratefully acknowledge these contributions and give particular thanks to the following individuals for their assistance and encouragement: Robert Johnson, Sam Ruinsky, Thomas Downs, Dee Dee Hickey, Kenneth Buettner, John Ottulich, Mary Hayes, Al Berr, Hope Alswang, and Patricia T. Smalley.

Janet Schneider
Executive Director
April 1989

Opposite: The People Wall, IBM Pavilion, 1964/ 65 World's Fair. Photograph by Gert Berliner.

Remembrance of Fairs Past

Robert Rosenblum

Top left: Aerial view, Hong Kong pavilion, 1964/65 Fair. Photography by Bob Golby, collection of The Queens Museum.
Top center: National Cash Register pavilion designed by Deeter & Ritchey for the 1964/65 Fair. Photograph by Peter M. Warner.
Top right: 1939 World's Fair plate, made by Tiffany and Company. Photograph by Phyllis Bilick, courtesy of The Queens Museum.
Above: John Atherton, *1939 World's Fair Poster.* Photograph by Jim Strong. Courtesy of The Queens Museum.
Opposite: Trylon and Perisphere, 1939/40 World's Fair. Photography collection of The Queens Museum.

For New Yorkers of my generation—I grew up in Manhattan during the Depression years—the thought of the New York World's Fair of 1939 is like the taste of Proust's *madeleine* or perhaps like deep analysis, a dizzy plunge into memory that, in this case, mixes one's own childhood with what now seems the childhood of our century. It was all, I recall, about the future; but then, what else would I be thinking about as my twelfth birthday approached in the summer of 1939? It was the moment, in fact, that I was anticipating eventual release from a Dickensian public school on Seventy-seventh Street and Amsterdam Avenue to the Elysian Fields of the High School of Music and Art, way up on Convent Avenue. I had already had quite a few precocious glimmers of the World of Tomorrow, which for me suddenly took material shape when I fell in love with the wraparound streamlin-

SINCLAIR DINOSAURS ON WAY TO N. Y. WORLD'S FAIR

ing that gave Cord cars a science-fiction modernity, or with the equally clean velocity of corner windows, open to the health-giving sun of Utopia, that marked the twin-tower Art Deco skyscrapers which loomed like cathedrals along Central Park West and carried *Brave New World* names like "The Century" and "The Majestic." And at a time when children could stroll more fearlessly in the city, I had already stumbled across the threshold of NYU's Museum of Living Art, down at Washington Square, and had seen pictures by Léger and Picasso, Miró and Mondrian that looked like blueprints for a future I hoped would be mine.

But all of these tremors of Things to Come were to turn, miraculously, into a total reality in the form of the Fair. Like something out of Buck Rogers or Flash Gordon, it was to land in Flushing Meadow in time for my own summer vacation of 1939. I remember the previews in the newspapers of extraterrestrial buildings that were called things like "Perisphere," "Futurama," "Trylon"; and as an early addict to roller coasters and amusement parks, I also stared in wonder at artists' renderings of strange new rides which would boggle the imagination of those who had only known the terrestrial pleasures of Coney Island and Palisades Amusement Park: the Bobsled, a version of greased lightning that would put wooden roller coasters back in a pre-industrial era, or the Parachute Jump, which promised the free-floating sublime, appropriate to the new era of space travel. Obsessed, I collected cuttings about the Fair from every imaginable source and then compiled them, with typed commentaries, for my grade-school scrapbook project, which I still preserve today in a plastic wrapper as a crumbling relic of my own

history and the world's.

And then, Eureka, the Fair opened! As soon as school closed, I rushed out to it on the Flushing IRT, being greeted, I recall, by the enchanted boardwalk of waving flags that led from the real-life grit of the subway to nothing less than the World of Tomorrow. And though I still find it hard to believe, I think I went out there by subway almost every single day of the summer holiday, rain or shine, returning exhausted and happy after sunset, having been dazzled by fireworks and colored beams against the night sky, but never so sated that I didn't long to return the next morning. For someone about to turn twelve and, I suspect, for everyone else too, the Fair was total, complete magic, and I couldn't rest content until I had seen absolutely everything not once, but again and again.

What a rush of memories! There was, above all, the exalting, cosmic Trylon and Perisphere that announced the arrival on our planet of a new religion I would readily have given my life for. And what about General Motors's "Futurama," the Fair's biggest hit? I remember how deliriously excited I was at those off moments when, say, the weather was so miserable or the time of day so offbeat that you could get right up the ramp without the usual two-hour wait; slip into a deeply comforting moving chair; listen to a wise, avuncular voice at your ear; and glide in rapture over a vista of Planet Earth, exploring a vision of promised technological happiness including, I'll never forget, an Amusement Park of the Future that featured a model of a roller coaster even more advanced than the Bobsled, made of—was I dreaming?—something like iridescent lucite.

And then there was the shock of modernity in art. I

Top left: General Motors pavilion, 1939/40 World's Fair. Photography collection of The Queens Museum.
Top right: Astral Fountain, 1964/65 Fair. Photograph by Peter Austin Leavens.
Above: Princess Grace of Monaco and her daughter Caroline with the manager of the Pepsi-Cola pavilion aboard the boat ride of "Its a Small World." Photograph courtesy of the Rare Books and Manuscripts Division, New York Public Library, Astor, Lenox, and Tilden Foundations.

remember to this day the thrill of the Finnish pavilion, whose fluid walls of billowing wood—designed, I learned much later, by the renowned Alvar Aalto—produced the same freeform delight I found in the first wiggling Mirós I had spied in Manhattan art museums; or the seductive invitation to surrealism's forbidden fruits provided by Salvador Dalí in the facade of his Dream of Venus pavilion, which, for reasons I can't dredge up, I never entered. (Was I too young to get into this mix of sex and Modern Art, or was it just too expensive?) Am I right in thinking that I really stopped in my tracks before a mural on the Hall of Pharmacy that, in my later life as an art historian, I realized had been executed after a project by de Kooning; or that my ears perked up with excitement at the sound of music accompanying a puppet show in the Hall of Medicine, music that turned out to be by Aaron Copland? With all the other siren songs, Modern Art, Modern Architecture, Modern Music beckoned me into the future.

Like the happiest of homeless people in Utopia, I somehow managed to live at, not visit, the New York World's Fair, still dreaming of it in my Manhattan bedroom. With the shrewdness of a street child, I soon learned that I could virtually have all my meals there free, by discovering which of the many concessions gave out samples. Just as RCA Victor seemed to have a complete set of its bound classical 78-rpm albums, any one of which could be heard at length for the asking, so, too, did the Heinz Dome have samples—could it possibly have been of *all* of its 57 varieties?—available for tasting. And for edible bounty, the Food Building was another free-for-all supermarket for children and paupers, where dessert could be picked up at the "Junket Folks" or, if you were old

enough, even a time-saving new product, instant coffee, could be savored. And if a free gulp of milk was wanted, there was always the Borden Company, with its "Roto-lactor" merry-go-round of hygienic cows being milked mechanically under the caring reign of its superstar, the photogenic Elsie the Cow, a prototype for Andy Warhol's bovine starlet from a far less ingenuous era, the 1960s.

As for technology, it could conquer not only archaic chores like milking cows, but also washing dishes in modern kitchens. At the Westinghouse Building (competing with General Electric), I often watched a hilarious skit that involved two women who demonstrated the before-and-after of mechanized happiness. One was a comedienne, à la Joan Davis, who, up to her shoulders in suds, frantically and clumsily washed—and often broke—a staggering load of glasses, china, and flatware. During this slapstick routine, the other housewife enjoyed the blessings of machine-made leisure while a Westinghouse dishwasher took care of her household duties, permitting her to read, in extravagant comfort, a stack of magazines. (Do I remember the *Ladies Home Journal* in the pile?) Such was the women's liberation promised in 1939 by the prophets of the Machine Age!

There was other technological entertainment, too, in the Bell Telephone exhibit where you were permitted to enter a lottery and, should you be lucky enough to win, to be privileged to telephone long distance any place in the USA—a luxurious modern dream come true, the catch being that everybody could listen in to the winning phone call on the phones provided by Ma Bell. I still recall the goose pimples when I won at the draw, and the vast public humiliation when I couldn't think of any place farther

Top left: Africa pavilion, 1964/65 Fair, designed by Kahn & Jacobs. Photograph courtesy of Peter M. Warner.
Top right: Installation of Ellsworth Kelly's *Two Curves: Blue Red* on the exterior of the 1964/65 New York State pavilion. Photograph by the artist.
Above: Contents of the 1964/65 Westinghouse Time Capsule. Photograph courtesy of Peter M. Warner and Westinghouse Electric Corporation.

away to telephone than Connecticut, where my sister was summering at camp. Had I only been sophisticated enough to know someone in faraway California, a sure passport to glamour!

As for other entertainments, who could forget the scary moment when, wandering through the New York Amphitheater, I accidentally found an unlocked door that gave me illegal, unticketed access to, lo and behold, the prohibitively expensive (was it forty cents?) show of shows, Billy Rose's Aquacade. Suddenly, way down below, before my eyes, was the watery spectacle of Eleanor Holm, the central cog in a fabulous geometric wheel of gyrating aquabelles whose star-shaped, snow-flaked patterns echoed the great Busby Berkeley productions I thought could exist only in the two-dimensional fantasy of a movie envisioned in remote Hollywood.

Still more exotic, the Fair offered most of us, young and old, our first glimpses of countries that we had only seen or heard about in movies and school books. Who would bother to notice that Germany was absent, when Poland, Iraq, Venezuela, Australia, and every other country was there? And after seeing Japan, Italy, and the Soviet Union on parade together in this pageant of international harmony, I can begin to understand why many Americans still have trouble deciding who was fighting whom during World War II, which broke out, it seemed, on another planet just before Labor Day and only weeks before the Fair closed for the season in 1939, to reopen, minus the Soviet pavilion, in 1940.

Twenty-five years later, I returned to the New York World's Fair, again riding on the tracks of the same old Flushing IRT; but by 1964, everything else, from me to the

Top right: Coca-Cola pavilion at the 1964/65 Fair, designed by Welton Becket & Associates. Photograph courtesy of Welton Becket & Associates.
Top left: Monorail, designed by Walter Dorwin Teague Associates for the 1964/65 Fair. Photograph courtesy of Walter Dorwin Teague Associates.
Above: Continental Baking Company Building, 1939/40 Fair. Photograph by Bob Golby, collection of The Queens Museum.

twentieth century, had changed. The World of Tomorrow we had counted on in 1939 had evaporated together with Hiroshima, and only fools and hopeless provincials could look with wide-eyed hope at the future of modernity and the blessings of the Machine Age. Pop Art was only two years old, and its poker-faced ironies—if you can't lick it, join it—somehow set the stage for my own return to Flushing's version of Arcadia. I loved the 1964 Fair, too, but for the totally new reason that it provided an extravagant surplus of outrageous kitsch, where the collision of postwar realities and prewar fantasies gave one the choice of weeping or smiling. I chose to smile, and there was a lot to smile about. Did I dream it, or was there really a dead-serious movie in the Mormon pavilion about Life After Death, in which blessed souls were filmed ankle-deep in stage smoke? I recall yet another evangelical display about spiritual harmony and the peaceable kingdom which demonstrated its point by a zoo-like enclosure in which one could see cohabiting living specimens of a black man and a white woman together with the most oddball variety of house pets and farm animals, or has my memory gone over the edge? Then there was the meal I had at the African pavilion, which consisted entirely of dishes made with peanuts (peanut soup, chicken with peanut sauce, salad with peanut dressing, and peanut ice cream). And I remember, too, a building called the Hall of Free Enterprise, with a screen facade of a freestanding Greek Doric colonnade on whose architrave was inscribed, "The Greatest Good for the Greatest Number," a design that was either the last surviving insult to the ardent spirit of Machine-Age architecture, so fantasized at the 1939 Fair, or the first straw in the campier winds of

Top left: Walt Disney "feeding" the dinosaurs in the Ford pavilion, 1964/65 Fair. Photograph courtesy of the Walt Disney Company. © 1989 Walt Disney Company.
Top right: Puppeteers Bil and Cora Baird with writer Burt Shevelove rehearsing "Motor Blockettes" presented in 1964/65 at the Chrysler pavilion. Photograph by Russ, Kirk and McAuliffe, Inc. Courtesy of Peter M. Warner.
Above: Travelers Insurance Companies' 1964/65 pavilion, designed by Kahn & Jacobs. Photograph courtesy of Peter M. Warner.

Post-Modernism. The giggling never seemed to stop, even though there were such nods in the direction of right-thinking modernity as Philip Johnson's festive New York State pavilion, and more seriously, the murals Johnson commissioned for it from Andy Warhol, the *Thirteen Most Wanted Men,* which, proving too disturbingly real to survive the Fair's glut of superannuated American dreams, were whitewashed over.

The perfect comments, both grave and smiling, about this moment of disillusion came, in the mid- and late sixties, from James Rosenquist in his *F-111* wraparound mural and from Roy Lichtenstein in his own mural commentaries on the end of the era of progress, *Preparedness* and *Peace through Chemistry.* The Age of Innocence had disappeared forever, mine and the century's. Today, twenty-five more years later, even the ironies of the sixties seem remote, replaced by a World of Tomorrow too chilling to contemplate, except perhaps as safely embalmed at EPCOT, with its perfect but hollow simulation of the form and spirit of 1939. As for that form and spirit, I often think of these ghosts on the way to the airport or to Long Island, catching from a swiftly moving car the archaeological site of Flushing Meadow, where one can still see, miraculously surviving, like Roman temples after the fall, scattered, lonely buildings from both fairs that once symbolized the power of New York City and New York State. And way off in the distance, one can still glimpse from the Belt Parkway the spidery silhouette of the Parachute Jump, transported to Coney Island after its initial glory at the 1939 Fair and now left an inert, monumental ruin, at the edge of both land and sea.

Weegee (Arthur Felig) used a kaleidoscope to photograph the Unisphere. Photograph courtesy of UPI/Bettmann Newsphotos.

The People Wall,
IBM Pavilion, 1964/
65 World's Fair.
Photograph by Gert
Berliner.

From the Thirties to the Sixties: *The New York World's Fair in its own Time*

Morris Dickstein

Despite their sometimes blatant commercial goals, world's fairs are first of all happenings—social moments in the popular imagination. And if they are successful they become markers of historical time, like the capsules they bury in the ground that send messages, often frivolous ones, to the people of a distant and almost unimaginable future. As special events to be cherished and remembered, great fairs, like local ones, are pieces of popular culture, very much dependent on the excitement of crowds, on color, scale, and spectacle; on freakish feats of engineering or physical skill; on special effects of illusion and verisimilitude; on evoking a sense of the unusual, the marvelous, the wonderful.

For reasons of sheer scale and

expenditure, as well as its enduring place in popular affections, the World's Fair of 1939/40, "could claim to be the greatest exhibition ever held."[1] It achieved its powerful impact in many ways: the classically symmetrical ground plan, detested by most architecture critics; the color-coded zones, which turned the Fair into a large playland; the vast size and attractive symbolism of the Trylon and Perisphere, with their geometrical simplicity. Above all, the Fair succeeded by imagining a future after a decade of Depression and scaling those wonders down to manageable size, including millions of trinkets and souvenirs. The Fair was a stunning piece of science fiction for an age poised at the brink of an economic and technological leap.

The most popular exhibits were notable for their brilliant effects of miniaturization. The Fair was full of breathtakingly detailed models of the World of Tomorrow. The General Motors "Futurama," contained, according to the 1939 guidebook, "approximately 500,000 individually designed houses; more than a million trees of eighteen species; and 50,000 scale-model automobiles, of which 10,000 are in actual operation over super-highways, speed lanes, and multi-decked bridges."[2] "Democracity," within the Perisphere, was a "symbol of a perfectly integrated futuristic metropolis pulsing with life and rhythm and music."[3] Con Edison's immense diorama of New York, the City of Light, a full block long and three stories high, used the effects of light, color, sound, and animation to play out a 24-hour day, including a thunderstorm, in just twelve minutes.

When people are asked what they liked about the 1939/40 Fair, they frequently say there was something "magical" about it, especially at night when dramatic lighting, ingenious color-patterns, and spectacular fireworks played to maximum effect. The continuous movement of vast numbers of people was itself part of the magic of the Fair—the always-long lines zig-zagging toward the "Futurama," the two long escalators leading up into the Trylon, the ramps of the Helicline descending from the Perisphere. Crowds were built into the Fair's mesmerizing geometry. It was the culmination of a decade fascinated by the crowd, the collective, from Ortega's *Revolt of the Masses* to Hitler's Nuremberg rallies, from Busby Berkeley's choreography to the great Depression crowd scenes in Frank Capra's films *American Madness* and *Meet John Doe*.

The Fair summarized the themes of a decade while envisioning a great leap forward. It cast a spell which is still vividly remembered; indeed, it remains *the* fair for many Americans. Despite the sharp attacks of many critics and intellectuals like Lewis Mumford, which began long before the Fair opened, despite the commercial disaster which kept it from paying back more than 20 cents on the dollar to its noteholders, the 1939/40 Fair retains its near-mythical status half a century later. Much of this legendary quality comes through in the strong concluding scenes of E.L. Doctorow's autobiographical novel, *World's Fair* (1985).[4] For Doctorow's protagonist, Edgar, a child growing up in a close-knit, enveloping Jewish family, the Fair provides an exotic peek at the outside world, a savory promise of freedom. It offers him some escape from home, family, neighborhood, and routine.

In two exciting visits to the 1939/40 Fair, the event becomes fraught with intimations of the boy's coming of age—as a sexual being, as an incipient (and unconventional) writer, and as a young man independent of his family, even somehow responsible for his family, which has suffered serious reverses during the Depression.

Seen through the eyes of a nine-year-old boy, most of the magic of the Fair can be found in the sideshow world of the amusement zone. But the "Futurama" enthralls young Edgar, as it did most other visitors, as a breathtakingly atmospheric ride over fantastic terrain, a science-fiction adventure rather than a sober-sided glimpse into the future. With "all the small moving parts, all the lights and shadows, the animation," he feels he is "looking at the largest most complicated toy ever made!"[5] By the end, despite his newly won maturity, his growing worldliness, he continues to see everything through a boy's sense of wonder, his keen eye for marvels.

After the privations of the Depression years, adults looked at the technology and consumer goods displayed at the 1939/40 Fair with a similar sense of wonder. They marveled at the labor-saving machines that still were available only to the few; they were impressed by the new toys, by the miracle of television, by the pioneering color photographs displayed by Kodak, by the remarkable new synthetic fabrics like Nylon. Twenty-five years later, New York would try to recreate that magic, using a similar ground plan on the same site with some

Below, top and bottom: The wonders of electrical power were extolled in the Tower of Light pavilion's show designed by Robinson-Capsis-Stern Associates. These scenes depict home life "aglow" with modern electrical applicances. Photographs courtesy of Alfred Stern.

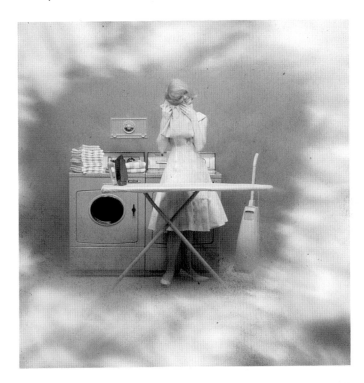

of the same exhibitors. The vapid slogan "Peace Through Understanding" took the place of "Building the World of Tomorrow"; the steel-ribbed Unisphere, a kind of skeleton world, replaced the Trylon and Perisphere; and a well-executed but far less magical version of "Futurama" tried hard to live up to the old Fair's most popular exhibit.

There were many reasons why the 1964/65 World's Fair fell so far short of its predecessor. Both took place on the cusp of a new era—the World War II years and America's Vietnam period—but the differences were immense. The coming of World War II merely postponed the consumer culture foreshadowed by the 1939/40 Fair. Indeed, the war shifted American industry into high gear, accelerated both technical research and mass production, and succeeded where the New Deal had failed: it brought the Depression to an end. In 1940 there were still almost 10 million Americans unemployed, down from 13 million at the height of the Depression. After the war, the American economy dominated a ravaged world. "In 1947," Godfrey Hodgson observed, "with postwar recovery under way everywhere, the United States produced about one half of the world's manufactures: 57 percent of its steel, 43 percent of its electricity, 62 percent of its oil. It owned three quarters of the world's automobiles and was improving on that show by manufacturing well over 80 percent of the new cars built in the world that year."[6]

This was the period when ordinary Americans developed their love affair with the automobile, and helped create the world of "Highways and Horizons" which GM had limned and promoted at the Fair. The "Futurama" had predicted that a staggering 38 million cars would be on the road by 1960; in fact there were 61 million.[7] Previous fairs, whatever their historical pretexts, had always in some part been celebrations of the city. These large expositions, almost cities in themselves, had enabled London and Paris, even Chicago, to declare themselves crossroads of the world, while smaller cities like Buffalo and Brussels, Philadelphia and New Orleans, San Francisco and St. Louis had asserted their own claims to the world's attention. But General Motors' homage to the highway and the automobile, which appealed so strongly to American individualism and love of mobility, foreshadowed not the antiseptic, utopian city portrayed in the "Futurama," but the flight from the city, the city in decay within a suburbanized nation.

Despite the vast social problems that came along with urban blight, the years from 1945 to 1965 were an oasis of middle-class affluence in the United States. The end of the war let loose a tremendous appetite for consumer goods that had been stifled since the early years of the Depression. The returning soldiers raised larger families in newly constructed housing, bought not only cars, but television sets, washing machines, record-players. "The booming economy enabled millions of Americans to take part in the burgeoning consumer culture," the historian William E. Leuchtenburg noted. "The economy not only turned out an abundance of goods for the American consumer but gave him more leisure to enjoy them."[8]

America's gain in leisure time and disposable income was not for everyone, but, as the 1939/40 Fair had predicted, at least some of the fruits of the new technology became almost universally available. The American experience became an experiment in the mass-production of upper-class amenities. In May 1935, when the New Deal created the Rural Electrification Administration, nine out of ten American farms still had no electricity. "Farmers, without the benefits of electrically powered machinery, toiled in a nineteenth-century

Below: Aerial view of the parking lot at the 1964/65 Fair. Photograph courtesy of Peter Warner.

Right: The GM-X, one of three experimental cars of the future displayed at the General Motors "Futurama." Photograph courtesy of the Rare Books and Manuscripts Division, New York Public Library, Astor, Lenox, and Tilden Foundations.

world," Leuchtenburg observed. "Farm wives, who enviously eyed pictures in the *Saturday Evening Post* of city women with washing machines, refrigerators, and vacuum cleaners, performed their backbreaking chores like peasant women in a preindustrial age."[9] In the postwar period the farmers would eventually enjoy almost all the comforts of city life, but there would be many fewer farmers to appreciate them. The same industrialization that made farming more efficient also diminished the need for manpower and helped eliminate many family farms. For many, "progress" proved to be an ambiguous development.

Meanwhile, foreign competition substantially reduced America's position in the world market. In 1939, the gigantic displays by Ford, General Motors, and Chrysler were the anchors of the Fair. Situated directly opposite the New York City Building and the Trylon and Perisphere, on the central axis of the Fair, they were the places everyone visited first. Their location and popularity reflected the auto industry's dominant standing in both America's and the world's economy. At the 1964/65 Fair, the Big Three auto-makers *seemed* to occupy the same ground, but this was a dangerous illusion that could not last long. Even as companies like Volkswagen were eating into the American market, a young muckraker and consumer advocate, Ralph Nader, published a book in 1965 called *Unsafe at Any Speed*, which indicted the American auto industry for its poor standard of workmanship, its arrogance, and its carelessness about safety.

Just as U.S. Steel, which donated the 1964/65 Fair's Unisphere, would lose its place in the world steel market, the auto companies would see their position erode both at home and abroad. Despite its effort to recapture the futuristic orientation of its predecessor, the 1964/65 Fair really came at the end of an era, the very era foreshadowed so uncannily

by the earlier event. If 1939 was the promise, 1964 was the fulfillment—but a fulfillment already crumbling as the crowds made their way through Flushing Meadow.

Though no one knew it at the time, by 1964 the future had already happened; the postwar boom was running out of gas. Some of this decline was due to foreign competition, some to the very standard of living already achieved—union shops, decent wages, good working hours—and some to poor management, bad design, and a loss of entrepreneurial imagination; the shoddy results could be seen at the 1964/65 Fair itself. But some of the shortcomings of the Fair can be traced to the very corporate ideal of progress and profits that the event celebrated. Though the Fair took place chronologically in the sixties, it was infused throughout with the conservative spirit of the 1950s. The planners were older men like Robert Moses and Walt Disney, both nearing the end of their careers, or younger men who were following a ground plan that had been laid out twenty-five years earlier.

The 1964/65 Fair took little account of the changes that had transformed American society and its values since the previous exposition. Indeed, it was far more conservative in outlook than the 1939/40 Fair. The original "Futurama," for example, had been roundly criticized for paying little heed to religion in its picture of the technological utopia; for the 1940 version, the designer, Norman Bel Geddes, added 200 churches to his enormous model. In a remarkable concession to matters religious, in 1964 Robert Moses offered land rent-free to religious denominations that would build pavilions at the Fair, and at least nine did, including the Billy Graham organization and the Vatican. There was also a Protestant Center, a Mormon pavilion, a Christian Science pavilion, and a Russian Orthodox church.

Below: Fifty high-ranking officials from twelve African nations visted the Fair. Photograph courtesy of the Rare Books and Manuscripts Division, New York Public Library, Astor, Lenox, and Tilden Foundations.

Right: Art Buchwald performing with folk dancers at the Republic of New Guinea pavilion. Photograph courtesy of the Rare Books and Manuscripts Division, New York Public Library, Astor Lenox, and Tilden Foundations.

As one contemporary critic commented: "In the midst of the fevered huckstering at the 1964/65 New York World's Fair, religion has returned, no longer divine, no longer master of events, but suppliant, competing hard with other exhibitors in selling a unique product."[10] This phenomenon no doubt was an offshoot of the famous "religious revival" of the 1950s—the symptom perhaps of a loss of identity and of a nuclear Age of Anxiety—an outbreak of suburban "togetherness" in which church membership boomed with no noticeable rise in piety or spirituality.[11]

As religion returned to the Fair, the fleshpots of Babylon were banished. The amusement zone which had sprung up spontaneously on the outskirts of Philadelphia's Centennial Exhibition of 1876 and was finally integrated into Chicago's Great Columbian Exposition of 1893—the fair that had given the world the Ferris Wheel as its answer to Paris's Eiffel Tower—had been so sanitized by Moses in 1964 that it became an object of universal derision. Yet Moses was perhaps responding to the genteel, respectable critics of the 1939/40 Fair—critics who differed markedly from Doctorow's pubescent hero in their feelings about Oscar the Amorous Octopus and Billy Rose's moist "Aquacade" showgirls. One of them, Sidney M. Shalett, had summed up the 1939/40 Fair in *Harper's* as "the paradox of all paradoxes: It was good, it was bad; it was the acme of all crazy vulgarity, it was the pinnacle of all inspiration. It had elements of nobility, features so breathtakingly beautiful you could hardly believe they were real. It also had elements of depravity and stupidity, features that were downright ugly. It proved that Man . . . in the midst of the age's finest technological wonders, could display incorrigible preferences for such low pastimes as peep shows and tippling."[12]

No doubt remembering such

attacks on the earlier Fair, when, as New York City Park Commissioner, he had been simply the Fair's landlord, Moses was rumored to have "inspected the costume of every waitress, every flamenco singer and Balinese dancer and Hawaiian hula-hula girl. By his ukase even the puppets at *Les Poupées de Paris* had to don brassières."[13] The puritanism of the old Progressive reformer held firm until the attendance figures brought Moses face-to-face with financial catastrophe. By the Fair's second season, there were discothèques with go-go dancers and many more carnival-style booths, though, typically, Moses refused to acknowledge that he had given in.[14]

Moses was certainly no P.T. Barnum; it would be an understatement to say that he lacked the popular touch.[15] As with many reformers, "the people" were but an abstract object of Moses's benefactions—*he* knew what they wanted—and some of his public works (like Jones Beach, which was inaccessible by mass transit) were designed to keep the rabble out. As a road-builder and slum-clearer he seemed to take an almost perverse pleasure in plowing through people's homes, even in decimating whole neighborhoods—for their own benefit, of course. By the 1960s, Moses's ideas of development were increasingly under siege. The Fair would be their last monument, and their Waterloo, at least until the unbridled money and real estate boom of the 1980s. Moses thought of this Fair as the culmination of his career, but many elected officials considered it a way of detaching him gracefully from his numerous city and state jobs. To a remarkable extent, Moses's crusty personality dominated the publicity for the Fair. His biographer, Robert Caro, speculates that this looming, outsized figure in the foreground, "a figure not inviting but hostile, a figure of arrogance and controversy and rage," may have kept many from attending a fair they

Above: Pearl Bailey performed in Sid and Marty Krofft's "Les Poupées de Paris" musical revue. Bailey sported $15,000 worth of chincilla on her gown. The show consisted of 250 puppets. Photograph courtesy of Peter M. Warner.

Right: To increase revenues and attendance, Moses added amusement attractions for the 1965 season of the Fair. Go-go dancer Candy Johnson performed live at the Gay New Orleans Club on "Bourbon Street." Photographs courtesy of Photofest.

might otherwise have greatly enjoyed.[16]

It would be hard to find a better summary of the ideals of progress and development of the 1950s than in the 1964 successor to Bel Geddes's "Futurama." As in the earlier version, the ride lasted for fifteen minutes and covered almost a third of a mile. Sitting three abreast, visitors were conveyed across the surface of the moon, to the Antarctic, along the ocean floor, through the jungle, through a desert, and finally past the city of the future, as GM's designers envisioned it. At each stage the visitors could see GM's "machines of tomorrow" subduing the once-recalcitrant environment. A GM press release put it this way: "In six scenes along the Futurama ride GM shows how improvements in current technology may clear the way for man to enter, exist within and develop lands which lie unused today." The epitome of these machines could be observed in the jungle section, "a self-propelled road-builder which leaves an elevated superhighway in its wake," preceded by two tree-clearing machines using laser beams "to saw off the age-old trees at their base." The press handout goes on:

The road-builder is indeed a factory on wheels. Fully automated, it levels the ground, sets stanchions, casts and places the road-surface slabs and links each unit into the highway which emerges in its wake.

Follow-up vehicles install lighting, traffic control and railings to complete the express highway. . . .

The road-builder brings more than just a highway to the jungle. It brings a new way of life to an area that has long—and successfully—defied man's attempts to develop its natural resources and take advantage of its climate and fertile soil.

The roadway goes where it can serve most effectively. It provides an outlet for the jungle's products—its lumber, its minerals and chemicals, its produce and crops. It also provides a source of goods and materials needed by the area's people, industry, agriculture and commerce. . . . The road-builder brings more than a highway to the jungle; it brings progress and prosperity as well.

Even if we did not know today that the deforestation of the Amazon by predatory developers threatened the entire world's

Below: In the jungle environment of the "Futurama," the "jungle-road builder" was a "factory-on-wheels" and cut through the forest to create finished highways. Photograph courtesy of General Motors.

Opposite: "A trip to the moon" was another scene from the "Futurama." The "articulated crawler" was capable of moving across any terrain obstacle. Here, it transverses the moon's surface toward a communication center. Photograph courtesy of General Motors.

oxygen supply, this development scheme could still stand as a model of economic exploitation and a naive utopian faith in technology. It is the white man's vision of what Joseph Conrad in *Heart of Darkness* called the "blank places on the earth." Conrad's story amply provides us with the dark underside of this missionary zeal to civilize the jungle and turn it to profit.

Projected to be a block long, eighty-feet high, and operated by thirty men, this road-builder/Frankenstein—described by GM as "capable of producing from within itself one mile of four-lane, elevated superhighway every hour," leveling everything in its path—is a kind of mechanical version of Moses himself, the can-do master builder who cut such a wide swath through bureaucratic red tape and human opposition alike. This is a "Highways and Horizons" vision run amuck, with little actual relevance to the lives of spectators who took the ride on the 1964/65 "Futurama."

This remoteness was probably the main reason why the 1964/65 encore, though popular, touched people so much less deeply than the original had done. By 1964 the road-building dream of the first exhibit had in essence been achieved, thanks to the Federal Interstate Highway System of the Eisenhower years. The new "Futurama" set out to apply that vision to the dark places on the map—the South Pole, the sea, the jungle, the desert—an endeavor somewhat in the spirit of nineteenth- and early-twentieth-century fairs, which ethnologically stressed distant places rather than future times, a Dahomey village rather than the City of Tomorrow.[17] But observers in 1964 complained that they had no practical interest in exploring the moon, setting up shop in Antarctica or under the sea, or building their homes into the crag of a cliff. Even the city, which concluded the ride, struck some people as a futuristic nightmare dominated by layers of highways.

This urban vision was Le Corbusier's perfectly planned Radiant City, with centrally controlled traffic, little or no greenery, and not much evidence of human life despite the presence of 1,600 moving vehicles and 8,500 miniature figures.[18] One friendly critic wondered "why the people of the future would be so willing to court acrophobia on the mountaintop or claustrophobia in the vasty deep," but when he came to GM's city he had his answer, for that seemed an even worse place to live: "I saw no parks, no grass, no trees, though there may have been a few buried away on some sunless level below the soaring belts of concrete. It is a city engineered for machines but not designed for people, not for me."[19] Despite the ingenuity of the new "Futurama," it could not reach people where they lived, nor did it project a future that truly engaged them.

By 1964, such critics as Jane Jacobs and Paul and Percival Goodman had already begun to question the received wisdom of urban planning. They saw city neighborhoods not as slums to be cleared and traffic to be expedited, but as complex, delicate organisms full of precious street life, small businesses, vital ethnic and generational relationships, and intricate family patterns. In 1935, Lewis Mumford, in the spirit of the 1930s, had expressed the hope that the 1939 Fair would tell the world "the story of this planned environment, this planned industry, this planned civilization."[20] By the 1960s, with an anarchic exuberance that was very much against the spirit of the new Fair, a different kind of utopianism was coming into fashion. It was local and communitarian, suspicious of large-scale planning and regimentation, convinced that Small Is Beautiful, and that the ethos of development was blind to fundamental human needs. It preached participatory democracy and proclaimed its respect for individual difference and eccentricity. It spoke for the marginal and the excluded, sharing the concerns of the young civil rights movement and helping to light the way for the women's movement.

It was in this spirit that Bronx residents had tried to save their neighborhood from Moses's Cross-Bronx Expressway, that mothers with baby carriages had defended trees in Central Park against Moses's bulldozers, that Manhattanites had managed to stop two more Moses expressways from slicing across their borough. A new wind was blowing in America, in a different direction from the top-down planning of Robert Moses and the Fair which reflected his values.

The clearest sign of trouble came when the opening day of the Fair became a focus for civil rights demonstrations. CORE objected to the racial policies of some of the Fair's exhibitors, including particular corporations and states. It was also putting on pressure for passage of the federal Civil Rights bill, which had gotten through the House in February and was stalled by a filibuster on the Senate floor. (The deadlock was broken two weeks later.) With a keen eye for anti-Moses symbolism, the head of CORE's Brooklyn chapter, Isaiah Brunson, threatened a stall-in on all the newly built access roads leading to Flushing Meadow. "We're going to block every street that can get you anywhere near the World's Fair," said Brunson, "and give New York the biggest traffic jam it's ever had." According to *Life*, Moses was prepared. Police virtually lined the roads: "Long lines of wreckers waited beside the expressways. A helicopter, capable of lifting cars from the roadway, stood ready. Police on foot were posted at regular close intervals, ready to pounce on anyone who paused."[21] It was as if Moses was determined to implement the scenario for traffic control that was on display in the "Futurama."

Moses, it turned out, was *too* well

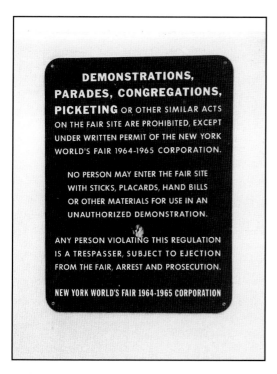

DEMONSTRATIONS, PARADES, CONGREGATIONS, PICKETING OR OTHER SIMILAR ACTS ON THE FAIR SITE ARE PROHIBITED, EXCEPT UNDER WRITTEN PERMIT OF THE NEW YORK WORLD'S FAIR 1964-1965 CORPORATION.

NO PERSON MAY ENTER THE FAIR SITE WITH STICKS, PLACARDS, HAND BILLS OR OTHER MATERIALS FOR USE IN AN UNAUTHORIZED DEMONSTRATION.

ANY PERSON VIOLATING THIS REGULATION IS A TRESPASSER, SUBJECT TO EJECTION FROM THE FAIR, ARREST AND PROSECUTION.

NEW YORK WORLD'S FAIR 1964-1965 CORPORATION

Left: Sign at the entrance to the Fair prohibiting demonstrations, parades, congregations and pickets. Photograph by Peter M. Warner.

Below, top: CORE (Congress on Racial Equality) demonstrators on opening day of the 1964/65 Fair protested the racial policies of some of the Fair's exhibitors. Photograph by Peter M. Warner.

Below, bottom: CORE demonstrators in front of the New York City pavilion on opening day at the 1965/65 Fair. Photograph courtesy of the New York Daily News.

prepared. Brunson had promised two thousand cars, but barely a handful materialized. The hapless leader was stranded back in Brooklyn because he had neglected to arrange for a car to carry him to his own demonstration. At the Fair itself, some three hundred protestors were arrested in sit-downs, including CORE's national director, James Farmer, but New York's roads had never been clearer, for most people elected simply to stay away. Attendance on opening day was under fifty thousand, only a fraction of what Moses had expected.

What all of this added up to was that despite its international theme, the Fair was in many ways a piece of white-bread America—religious, conservative, middle-class—plunked down in the heart of ethnic New York. To the dismay of civil rights leaders, there was not a single black or Puerto Rican on the Fair's administrative staff of two hundred, and few were employed, even in menial posts, around the building.[22] The whole enterprise was a throwback to a more homogeneous era in which blacks, like slums and other "social problems," were kept out of sight and out of mind. Any hint of inequality, conflict, or injustice was excluded from the social purview of the Fair.

As a result, the Fair became a focus for the new sixties style of protest and confrontation, especially after President Lyndon Johnson sharply escalated involvement in Vietnam early in 1965, sending in American ground troops and initiating daily bombing raids over North Vietnam. Just as World War II had intervened to alter the mood and meaning of the 1939/40 Fair, America's Vietnam War, with its overpoweringly sophisticated weaponry and logistical support, shed a new light on the technological utopia of the second Fair, with its theme of "Peace Through Understanding." By the time the Fair closed late in 1965, the nation was caught up in demonstrations far more extensive and impassioned than those the Fair had seen on its opening day. And this, too, spilled over into the Fair.

Notwithstanding the economic crisis of the thirties and the prosperity of the postwar years, the fairgoers of the mid-sixties found it much harder to believe in Progress than had their predecessors of 1939. The genie was out of the bottle: not everyone shared the fruits of progress in equal measure, nor had technology managed to solve all our problems; indeed, it had created many new problems, such as pollution, radioactive waste, and a whole new machinery of death. This news was slow to reach the planners of the 1964 General Electric pavilion, who hired Walt Disney to create a series of animated tableaux demonstrating the benefits of electricity since the 1880s. While an audience of 250 people revolved from stage to stage on an enormous carousel, they were shown six scenes of lifelike creatures with computerized movements, demonstrating how the American home and family had been transformed by electrical energy. (The idea was borrowed from the Electric Utilities exhibit of 1939.)

Elsewhere in the building, the public could gaze down on a dramatic demonstration of thermonuclear fusion, detonated every fifteen minutes. Nuclear power was presented as yet another facet of the benign possibilities of technology, like highways through the jungle. There's a risk, of course, in taking the Fair's exhibits too seriously, yet they do express the assumptions of the prevailing entrepreneurial culture of the 1950s, with its unlimited faith in progress through development, a faith that seems at best naive to us today, if not actually sinister or dangerous.

If the Fair was conservative in its political and social outlook, it was even more conservative aesthetically. The early, highly stylized Mickey Mouse had

been a special favorite of intellectuals in the 1930s, when Disney's cartoons were considered daringly imaginative examples of "pure cinema." But by the 1960s—he would die in 1966—Disney had become an establishment figure, the creator of Disneyland and the producer of a long-running television series. Moreover, he had long been devoted to creating what Richard Schickel calls "human simulacra," waxworks-like figures that could move, talk, and even sweat. The most famous of these was his Lincoln, reciting excerpts from the Gettysburg Address in the Illinois pavilion—in some ways the epitome of all that was wrong with the Fair, a fair that had tried so hard to keep flesh under wraps. As Schickel put it:

Disney, caught in the grip of his technical mania and protected by his awesome innocence about aesthetic and philosophical matters, had brought forth a monster of wretched taste which, for all the phony reverence and pomposity surrounding its presentation, leaves one in a state of troubled tension. Are we really supposed to revere this contraption, this weird agglomeration of wires and plastic . . . ?[23]

Like some of Disney's other inventions for the Fair, the Lincoln would eventually wind up at Disneyland in Anaheim, California—just the kind of costly, isolated theme park that would help make world's fairs obsolete.[24] Garry Wills states that the Disney version is a characteristically American way of looking at the past: "One must reject historical record for historical fantasy, fact for parable. . . . It is a safe past, with no sharp edges to stumble against."[25] To Wills, this was the simplified past espoused so effectively by Ronald Reagan, who until 1962 was honing his political skills as a spokesman for General Electric, even living in GE's all-electric demonstration house.

But the aesthetics of the Fair went far beyond Disney's eerie simulations. The Board of Design of the 1939 Fair had done much to give it a unified, harmonious look. "Replicas of historical buildings and extremely traditional structures were outlawed, except in the Government Zone and the Amusement Area," notes Stanley Appelbaum in his introduction to a collection of 155 photographs of the Fair.[26] Quite the opposite was true in 1964, when every exhibitor could build as he liked, and kitsch was king.

Kitsch had always been one of the delights and drawbacks of large expositions. Since most fair structures are torn down, architects have often used them to make unusual statements, sometimes boldly futuristic, sometimes wildly whimsical, sometimes crassly promotional. It's sobering to think that the decade which began with the Chrysler Building could come to an end with a building topped by a huge cash register and another whose exterior imitated the packaging of Wonder Bread. Yet these two architectural fantasies amused visitors to the 1939/40 Fair. Could Andy Warhol's *Brillo Boxes* be far behind?

One of the few elements of contemporary art that made it into the 1964/65 Fair was Pop Art, including works by Roy Lichtenstein, James Rosenquist, Robert Rauschenberg, and Andy Warhol. But even this rare feature of sixties culture did not get by unscathed, for Warhol's *Thirteen Most Wanted Men* was taken down shortly before the Fair opened. Perhaps it was too unpleasant a reminder that there *were* social problems in a great American city, something the Fair had done its best to suppress.

One reason this Pop Art was thoroughly overshadowed was that, as several observers remarked, the Fair itself was a gigantic piece of Pop Art. Eric Salzman made this point in an article devoted to the Fair. He found the enterprise loud, expensive, shoddy, and commercial but also immensely entertaining, full of showmanship and fakery, devoted not to art but to gimmicky "environments" and odd curios that made up as much of a mishmash as

Below: National Cash Register Company pavilion, 1939/40 Fair, designed by Walter Dorwin Teague. Photograph by Bob Golby, collection of The Queens Museum.

Right: Designed by Skidmore & Owings, the Continental Baking Company Building at the 1939/40 Fair housed the Wonder Bakery. Photography collection of The Queens Museum.

the architecture. "The Pop Art Fair is probably the biggest Curio and Junk Shop Mart in history. It is certainly the Miscellany of All Time and it undoubtedly sets some kind of world's record for ineffective ingenuity employed at displaying useless and gaudy wares."[27] Some of these wares have become collector's items, treasured memorabilia of the 1964/65 Fair, but without the cachet and commercial value that has accrued to trinkets from the 1939/40 Fair.

The egregious setting of Michelangelo's *Pietà*, behind a bullet-proof plastic shield, with viewers drifting by on a moving ramp, evoked some of the most vinegary criticisms of the 1964/65 Fair. But many of the objections were far too solemn and apocalyptic as if the statue had been irretrievably besmirched by its sideshow appeal. The *Pietà* at the Fair was not unlike Jenny Lind sponsored by Barnum, or Sarah Bernhardt performing in French under a tent in rural Texas, or the *Mona Lisa* with a mustache—a satirical mixture of mass and class, a half-intended thumb in the eye of high art. It represented Culture with a capital C, just as Disney's Lincoln was History.

The wonderful IBM pavilion by Saarinen and Eames, a flattened Fabergé egg nesting on the branches of steel trees, was a witty take-off on architecture as significant expression, the kind of thing that could happen only at a fair. This kind of playfulness has since become a key feature of what is called Post-Modernism—a travesty of high art and high seriousness, replete with historical quotation, including a return to some of the gaudy ornamentation that preceded the triumph of the International Style. Whether the Fair is called kitsch, or Pop, or Post-Modern, the carnival effect is the same. The 1939 Fair sought a unified style and a streamlined modern look consistent with its futuristic theme. Many found the effect quite magical: a new world opened up for them. The 1964/65 Fair settled for diversity, kitsch, and contradiction. Many of its exhibits were actually backward-looking, a celebration of progress already achieved. Few found the effect enchanting. Many found it vulgar.

Calculated and commercial as it was, the 1964/65 Fair today looks like the product of a more innocent age, the last gasp of the postwar era of confidence and complacency. The political explosions of the 1960s, the challenges to old ideas of progress, the new concerns about the environment and the quality of life, as well as America's growing economic problems and waning position in the world quickly turned the Fair into history and made it seem anachronistic.

The Fair was also one of the last of the gargantuan international expositions, the bitter end of a century of world's fairs that have now given way to expensive theme parks, trade shows, and amusement parks that are geared to separate audiences and have even less to offer aesthetically than Moses's Fair did. Television shows are now the corny expositions that aim to bring people together, that satisfy their curiosity about the world beyond their lives. People no longer have to *go* places; the world comes to them.

Yet this new form of popular culture actually reifies the atomization of the audience and its social divisions. Everyone is plugged into a separate box, and the sphere of public culture has been drastically diminished. For all their displays of technology, the world's fairs belonged to the horse-and-buggy era of mass culture, when entrepreneurs still staged live events and corporations hawked their wares like medieval vendors on market day. The world has changed, but the same doubts and confusions that once alienated people from the Robert Moses Fair have turned it, like the man behind it, into an object of nostalgia and affection.

Below: Walt Disney "feeding" the dinosaurs in the Ford pavilion's "Magic Skyway" designed by Walt Disney Imagineering. Photograph courtesy of The Walt Disney Company. © 1989 Walt Disney Company.

Right: Pope Paul VI and President John F. Kennedy with replica of the *Pietà*, July 2, 1963. The Pontiff agreed to lend the original statue to the Fair. Photograph courtesy of the Rare Books and Manuscripts Division, New York Public Library, Astor, Lenox, and Tilden Foundations.

1964

Former-president Herbert Hoover died at age 90.

Three civil rights workers murdered in Mississippi.

Civil Rights Act of 1964 enacted; protects voting right and prohibits racial discrimination in housing and employment.

President Lyndon Baines Johnson named *Time's* "Man of the Year."

Martin Luther King, Jr., awarded Nobel Peace Prize.

Jean Paul Sartre awarded Nobel Prize for literature.

Reader's Digest had the largest magazine circulation with a readership of 14,512,673, followed by *T.V. Guide* and *McCall's*.

The number one hit song was *I Wanna Hold Your Hand* by The Beatles.

The Beatles performed on "The Ed Sullivan Show" and toured the United States.

The best selling books were *The Spy Who Came in From the Cold* by John Le Carre and *On Her Majesty's Secret Service* by Ian Fleming (fiction); and *The Feminine Mystique* by Betty Friedan (non-fiction).

My Fair Lady voted best picture Academy Award; Julie Andrews named best actress for *Mary Poppins,* and Rex Harrison named best actor for *My Fair Lady.*

Other movies released were *Dr. Strangelove, A Hard Day's Night,* and *Lord of the Flies.*

Fiddler on the Roof won Tony Award for best musical and *The Subject was Roses* won Tony for best play.

Robert Rauschenberg won first prize at the Venice Biennale.

Right: President Lyndon B. Johnson at the opening ceremonies of the 1964 Fair. Photograph courtesy of Peter M. Warner.
Far right: Shown (from left): Fair Corporation President Robert Moses, Mayor Robert Wagner, and President John F. Kennedy viewing a model of the 1964/65 Fair. Although Kennedy was assassinated in November 1963 he was an instrumental supporter of the Fair effort.

1965

President Johnson ordered large-scale bombing of North Vietnam.

Malcolm X assassinated in New York.

Medicare and Voting Rights Act of 1965 enacted.

Pope Paul VI visited New York, October 4.

General William Westmoreland named *Time's* "Man of the Year."

The number one hit song was *Wooly Bully* by Sam the Sham and the Pharoahs.

Bob Dylan, The Rolling Stones, The Beatles, The Supremes, Herman's Hermits, The Beach Boys, and The Byrds all had hit records.

The best selling books were *The Source* by James A. Michner (fiction); and *How to be a Jewish Mother* by Dan Greenberg (non-fiction).

The Sound of Music was voted best picture Academy Award; Julie Christie was named best actress for *Darling*, and Lee Marvin was named best actor for *Cat Ballou*.

Other movies released included *Help!*, *A Patch of Blue*, *The Sandpiper* and *Dr. Zhivago*.

Man of La Mancha won Tony Award for best musical and *Marat/Sade* won Tony for best play.

Right: Ed Sullivan and the Beatles, Walter's International Wax Museum. 250 life-like figures were displayed at the Museum, the largest was a 20 × 30 foot recreation of Leonardo Da Vinci's *Last Supper*. Photograph courtesy of the Rare Books and Manuscripts Division, New York Public Library, Astor, Lenox, and Tilden Foundations.

Time Capsules, created by Westinghouse as "comprehensive crosssection[s] of today's civilization," were designed to affirm each fair's role as a microcosm of cultural values. The first of these cylinders was deposited on the grounds of the Westinghouse pavilion on September 23, 1938, six months prior to the opening of the 1939/40 Fair. At the 1964/65 Fair a second Time Capsule was created to reflect developments in society and culture in the intervening twenty-five years. The selection of the contents was made democratically, involving a selection committee as well as solicitations from Fair visitors. On October 16, 1965, this capsule was buried beside the 1938 version. Both remain in Flushing Meadow Park today, noted with a marker. The contents of the 1965 capsule were:

bikini
Polaroid camera
plastic wrap
electric toothbrush
tranquilizers
ball-point pen
molecular block

50-star American flag
superconducting wire
box of detergent
transistor radio
fuel cells
electronic watch
antibiotics
contact lenses
reels of microfilm
credit cards
ruby laser rod
ceramic magnet
filter cigarettes
Beatles record
irradiated seeds
freeze-dried foods
rechargeable flashlight
synthetic fibers
heat shield from Aurora 7
Revised Standard Version of the Bible
film history of the USS Nautilus
fiber-reinforced material
film identity badge
material from Echo II satellite
computer memory unit
pocket radiation monitor
graphite from first nuclear reactor
Vanguard satellite radio transmitter
container for carbon-14
tektite
pure zirconium
desalted Pacific Ocean water
birth-control pills
pyroceramic baking dish
plastic heart value
Official Guide to New York World's Fair
photographs of important events.

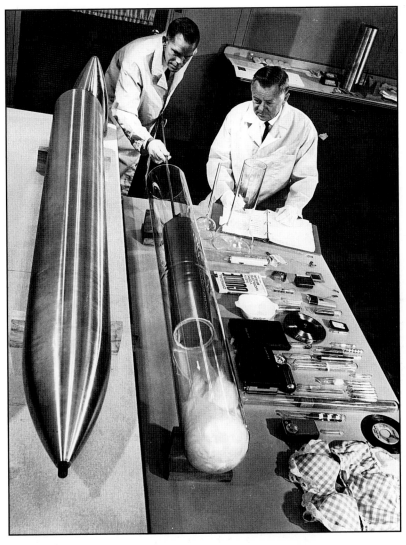

Left: Scientists at Westinghouse Corporation loading the contents of the Time Capsule, 1965. Photograph courtesy of Westinghouse Electric Corporation, Pittsburgh, and George Westinghouse Foundation, Wilmerding, Pennsylvania.

Below, left: Westinghouse Time Capsules displayed at the Westinghouse pavilion. Photograph courtesy of the Rare Books and Manuscripts Division, New York Public Library, Astor, Lenox, and Tilden Foundations and Westinghouse Electric Corporation.

Fair Corporation President Robert Moses posed with a model of the Unisphere. Photograph courtesy of Peter M. Warner.

Something for Everyone: *Robert Moses and the Fair*

Marc H. Miller

Certainly no person had a greater effect on the 1964/65 New York World's Fair than the Fair Corporation President, Robert Moses. When he took control of the Fair in May 1960, the seventy-year-old Moses was nearing the end of a remarkable career as New York City's master planner and builder. He had achieved a legendary stature in the city—the creator of more than 700 city parks, seven major bridges, virtually all of the city's expressways and parkways, dozens of public housing projects, and city landmarks like the United Nations headquarters and the New York Coliseum. His very agreement to become President of the World's Fair Corporation gave the fledgling enterprise instant credibility. Throughout its existence, the

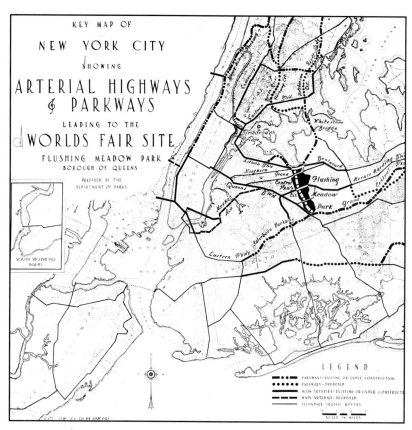

KEY MAP OF

NEW YORK CITY

SHOWING

ARTERIAL HIGHWAYS
& PARKWAYS

LEADING TO THE

WORLDS FAIR SITE

FLUSHING MEADOW PARK
BOROUGH OF QUEENS

PREPARED BY THE
DEPARTMENT OF PARKS

SOUTH RICHMOND
INSERT

LEGEND

Fair's image was linked to the public's perception of its renowned and controversial President; indeed, Fair publicity often was purposely centered around Moses. The powerful and opinionated Moses influenced all aspects of the Fair, and he deserves much of the credit for the spectacle's assets and much of the blame for its failures.

Robert Moses's role in the 1964/65 World's Fair was rooted in his past as one of the key players in the successful New York World's Fair of 1939/40. As New York City's representative in dealing with the 1939 Fair Corporation, directed by Grover Whalen, Moses was responsible for the site preparation and for improving the roadways leading to the Fair. In 1935, when the forty-six year-old Moses became involved with the first New York fair, he was already a well-known personality, popular for his 1920s development of Jones Beach, a large and elegant ocean recreation area on Long Island. As New York City Park Commissioner, Moses embarked on an ambitious plan to build ten full-size public pools, and to provide Manhattan and Brooklyn with new zoos. As Chairman of the Triborough Bridge Authority, he completed the construction of the long-delayed bridge. His energetic road construction programs brought about the Meadowbrook Parkway in Long Island, the Grand Central Parkway in Queens, and Manhattan's East River Drive extension.

Although he was one of the earliest supporters of the 1939 World's Fair, Moses was nearly indifferent to the Fair itself, interested only in the event's potential to generate permanent civic improvements. With business, city, state, and federal government fully backing the Fair, he regarded the 1939 event as a convenient, high-budget, high-priority enterprise that he could latch onto for advancing his main business: park and roadway construction. While he described

Below, top: Four-level highway interchange, Whitestone and Van Wyck Expressways. The anticipated increase in vehicular traffic, due to the estimated number of visitors to both the 1939/40 and 1964/65 Fairs aided Moses in his plans for developing a system of new roads and bridges for New York City. Photograph courtesy of Peter M. Warner.

Below, bottom: The New York City Pavilion's Triborough Bridge and Tunnel Authority exhibit at the 1964/65 Fair, designed by Lester Associates. Photograph courtesy of Lester Associates, Inc.

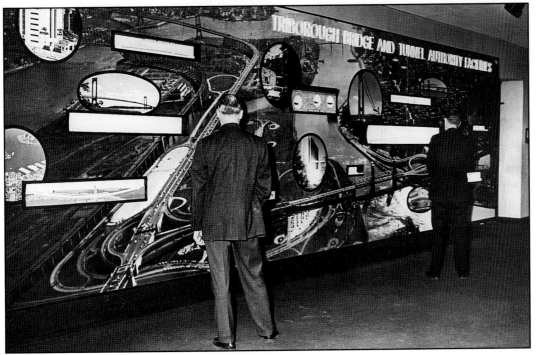

the decision to mount the 1939 World's Fair as a "miracle," in his more candid moments, he would call it a "gadget."[1]

Moses envisioned the 1939 Fair site as a permanent park. Flushing Meadow, a large tract of marshland near Flushing Bay in Queens, was the site of the Corona Dump. Piled high with mountains of burnt garbage, the 1,216-acre plot was offensive to the eye and nose. Yet Moses saw the location, at the geographic dead center of the New York metropolitan area, as an enormous opportunity. By 1932, he had already used part of the site for the Grand Central Parkway. When he was approached by advocates of the proposed New York World's Fair, the then-city Park Commissioner quickly fused their plans with his own park schemes, announcing that Flushing Meadow "was the only site in New York where they could get any cooperation from the Park Department."[2]

Moses's plan to use the Fair to furnish the city with a major new park garnered support for the World's Fair from New York Mayor Fiorello La Guardia. The lease that Moses negotiated in 1936 gave the Fair Corporation temporary use of Flushing Meadow in return for a long list of stipulated improvements; it was a masterful legal formulation, and granted Moses final approval over all Fair construction destined to be part of the post-Fair park. This included all roads, plantings, water and sewage pipes, electricity lines, and fountains, giving Moses virtual control of the entire Fair layout. While Moses was not part of the World's Fair Corporation, many of the landscape architects and designers from the Park Department had, with his encouragement, temporarily joined the Fair design staff. Among these was Gilmore D. Clarke, a member of the Fair's Board of Design, generally credited with working out the geometric *Beaux-Arts* plan used first for the Fair and then

Below, top: An aerial view from 1937 of the central portion of Flushing Meadow Park. Photograph by McLaughlin Air Service. Courtesy of the Department of Parks Photo Archive.

Below, bottom: Corona Dumps, 1933. Previous to its transformation into Flushing Meadow Park, this site was a tract of marshland that contained mountains of garbage. Photograph courtesy of the Triborough Bridge and Tunnel Authority.

Below: Shown (from left): Park Commissioner Robert Moses, 1939/40 Fair Corporation President Grover **Whalen**, and Mayor Fiorello La Guardia at the groundbreaking ceremony for Flushing Meadow Park, June 29, 1936. Photograph courtesy of the Fiorella H. La Guardia Archives, La Guardia Community College/The City University of New York.

Below: A 1965 view of the New York City pavilion, designed by Aymar Embury II, constructed originally for the 1939/40 Fair. It remains as the home of The Queens Museum and an ice-skating rink. Photograph by Ben Cohen, courtesy of the Department of Parks Photo Archive.

retained as the basic park layout.[3]

Moses took special interest in the construction of the New York City and New York State pavilions, scheduled to remain as permanent recreational facilities. The City pavilion was the only completely air-conditioned exhibition hall at the Fair, and it contained the world's largest indoor ice-skating rink as well as an exhibit area that would later be converted into a roller-skating rink. The handsome neo-classical structure with exterior glass brick walls was designed by Aymar Embury II, a Park Department architect who worked on Moses's public pools. The New York State pavilion was constructed as a water amphitheater, and during the Fair it housed Billy Rose's popular "Aquacade." Designed by the architectural firm of Sloan and Robertson, it was similar to the amphitheater Moses had built at Jones Beach, and in the post-Fair park the structure was planned to serve as both a theater and park pool.[4]

While the 1939/40 Fair served as Moses's "gadget" for developing Flushing Meadow Park, it also helped further his plans for new roads and bridges. With the advent of the affordable automobile, New York's transportation infrastructure needed an overhaul, and by 1930 Moses had a new roadway master plan. Flushing Meadow, at New York's center, was a natural hub for this network of roads. The traffic needs of the World's Fair were fused with Moses's own plans, helping him coalesce support and speed construction of key elements of his roadway program. The construction of the Bronx Whitestone Bridge and the Whitestone Expressway was linked to the Fair, and the project's opening-day ceremonies took place on the day the Fair opened. Under Moses's supervision, the Grand Central Parkway also was improved and extended.[5]

Moses chronicled his dream of constructing an ambitious new city park out of a mountain of ashes in *The*

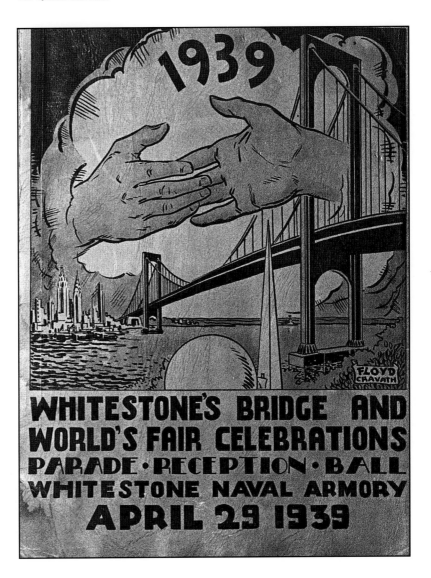

Below: Commemorative Journal for the opening ceremony of the Whitestone Bridge, April 29, 1939. This celebration coincided with the opening of the World's Fair. Collection of The Queens Museum. Photograph by Phyllis Bilick, courtesy of The Queens Museum.

Flushing Meadow Improvement, a monthly bulletin. To the north, the fountains and walkways constructed for the Fair would become part of a unique formal park layout he hoped would be "the Versailles of America." The south section of the park, with two artificial lakes, was to be relatively informal and natural in style.[6] Much of this transformation from garbage dump to "Versailles" took place in less than two years, as Moses's staff rushed to meet the opening-day deadline of the Fair. More work would follow the closing of the Fair.

In the contract Moses forged, the first $2 million of Fair profits was to go to the development of the park. Every detail of the transition from Fair site to city park was stipulated. But the Commissioner's grandiose plans for Flushing Meadow Park were dashed by the financial collapse of the World's Fair Corporation. When it turned out that Fair attendance was well below expectations, the anticipated profits turned to losses. The coming of World War II temporarily froze the park project; even finding funds to clean up was difficult, as post-Fair rubble threatened to transform Flushing Meadow back into a garbage dump.

Although Moses was disappointed by the 1939/40 Fair's financial failure and its consequences for Flushing Meadow Park, his involvement with the spectacle was a success. It capped a remarkably productive decade in which many of his youthful schemes for improving the park system and roadways of New York had come to rapid fruition. During the 1930s, Moses enjoyed wide popularity, personifying in real life the "Building the World of Tomorrow" theme that the Fair celebrated. Moses's roads, bridges, and large-scale recreation areas reconfigured modern life along the lines made possible by the proliferation of the automobile. Such Fair attractions as "Democracity," a model of an ideal community of the future, and General Motors's "Futurama,"

Below: Rendering of the proposed Flushing Meadow Park by John MacGilchrist, 1937. Photograph courtesy of the Department of Parks Photo Archive.

displaying a vision of America's highway system of tomorrow, illustrated a world that very closely resembled the one actually being built by Moses—a suburban metropolis in which work, living, and recreation all took place in separate areas connected by big superhighways.

Moses's successes from the 1930s consolidated his unprecedented political power, and his career as an urban planner and builder reached a feverish pace after World War II. In addition to constructing parks, roads, bridges, and tunnels, it was in the postwar years that Moses built public housing projects, the United Nations complex, and the New York Coliseum. Increasingly, however, Moses the tireless public servant was surrounded by controversy. As more of his plans for New York were becoming reality, critics began to challenge his vision for the city. With the spread of congestion and pollution, his unwavering allegiance to the automobile came under attack. So did his apparent indifference to the displacement of residents and the abolition of entire neighborhoods that his urban renewal schemes demanded. The argument was further fueled by Moses's self-righteous stubbornness and a contentious streak in his personality.

The seventy-year-old Moses's involvement in the 1964/65 Fair would be the last chapter of his remarkably productive career as a builder of New York. Still brimming with plans for the city, he saw the new Fair, which was budgeted at over $1 billion, as still another means of furthering his menu of civic improvements. His presidency of the Fair Corporation was his last hurrah. When it was over, his career was virtually completed.

To become head of the private Fair Corporation that would do substantial business with the city, Moses was required by law to resign his various city jobs. A dispute with Governor Nelson Rockefeller in 1962 led him to resign his state jobs as well. By the time his seven-year stint as President of the Fair Corporation ended in 1967, Moses was nearly eighty, and the only position he still held was as Chairman of the Triborough Bridge and Tunnel Authority. Even here he was soon forced to retire; his long—nearly fifty-year—reign as the *de facto* czar of city and downstate construction had come to an end.[7]

Even before he joined the Fair Corporation, Moses actively promoted initial plans for the Fair, first advanced in 1958 by Robert Koppel and others. Moses helped win city and state support for the enterprise, and accompanied Mayor Robert Wagner to Washington, D.C. to meet with President Dwight Eisenhower and solicit federal recognition for the enterprise. Although many observers objected to Moses replacement of Robert Koppel, the originator of the 1964 Fair concept, just as the Fair was becoming a reality, most people applauded his selection as Fair Corporation President. As a veteran of the 1939/40 Fair and as an insider with unquestionable administrative skills who could always meet a deadline, he seemed the ideal choice.

When Moses's management of the Fair proved controversial, it was in large part because of attitudes he had formed during his work in 1939. For the earlier Fair, Moses's role as city representative in dealing with the Fair Corporation had conditioned him to care only for the long-term civic benefits the Fair could produce. In those days, *The Flushing Meadow Improvement* bulletins, produced under his direction, carried articles analyzing previous world's fairs strictly in terms of the lasting improvements that they generated. From the perspective of those who loved fairs for their own sake, Moses was mixing up his priorities, ignoring his primary job of creating a successful Fair.

Moses admitted that his intention

Below: A 1961 aerial view of Flushing Meadow Park with chalk notations showing proposed highway improvements. This photograph was part of a survey of New York City by the Aero Photo Service in conjunction with the building of the Panorama of New York City. Photograph by Phyllis Bilick, collection of The Queens Museum.

Right: Aerial view of the 1939/40 World's Fair. Photograph courtesy of the Museum of the City of New York.

of generating permanent civic improvements was what led him to take on the presidency of the 1964/65 Fair, and he argued that this was the most valuable role a fair could play. Foremost was his desire to finish Flushing Meadow Park, a dream that had been thwarted by the financial difficulties that beset the 1939/40 Fair. Some further park improvements had been accomplished between 1946 and 1950, when Moses arranged for the former New York City pavilion to serve temporarily as the home of the United Nations while its Manhattan headquarters was still under construction. And in the early 1960s, Moses had begun construction of a 55,000-seat sports stadium in Flushing Meadow. Now, by way of his 1964/65 Fair presidency, Moses provided the park with outdoor sculpture and a Museum of Science and Technology; the profits anticipated were intended to provide a zoo and a botanical garden. As a builder in New York, Moses had learned to link projects, and the improvement of the roadways around Flushing Meadow would benefit not only the Fair, but the newly built sports stadium as well. Two other Moses projects—the Verrazano Narrows Bridge connecting Staten Island and Queens, and the Lincoln Center for the Performing Arts in Manhattan—were both scheduled to open in conjunction with the Fair, and all were to be part of an ambitious citywide celebration of the 300th anniversary of New York.[8]

Moses's overriding concern to use the Fair led him to scratch a proposal by the esteemed modernist architect Gordon Bunshaft, whom he himself had appointed as head of the design committee. Bunshaft proposed housing all the Fair exhibits in a gigantic donut-shaped pavilion (a plan similar to Baron Haussmann's for the 1867 Paris World's Fair). The huge structure would have cost the Fair Corporation millions, and countervailed Moses's plan to maximize Fair profits by

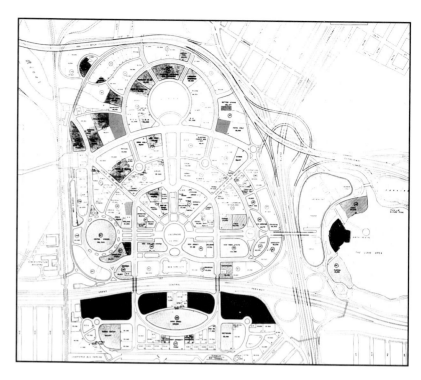

minimizing construction. As the man who had first approved Gilmore Clarke's design for Flushing Meadow Park, conceived originally as the layout for the 1939 Fair, Moses insisted that the new Fair conform to the readymade site. From his perspective, by having each participant in the Fair build his own pavilion, and by reusing the park's roadways, fountains, and underground infrastructure, the Fair Corporation could increase profits for post-Fair uses. This view did not sit well with the design committee; its members sought to create an original *new* Fair. In frustration, Bunshaft and others resigned.

The 1939/40 Fair had been marked by a precise intellectual vision and a clear, coherent program. Under the management of Fair President Grover Whalen and its theme committee, the Fair was structured around a single idea: "Building the World of Tomorrow." To successfully further the concept, the Fair Corporation constructed its own theme pavilions and exhibits, predicting future developments in communications, travel, and public health. Corporate pavilions too were expected to follow the World of Tomorrow theme. A central design

Above: Confidential space allocation plan, 1964/65 Fair. To save money, the layout of the Fair conformed to the 1939/40 Fair's configuration. Photograph courtesy of the Rare Books and Manuscripts Division, New York Public Library, Astor, Lenox, and Tilden Foundations.

committee assured visual unity, carefully working out a set of rules that all Fair participants were required to follow.

The 1964/65 Fair took an opposite approach. While Moses's decision to minimize central control of the Fair reflected the financial considerations related to his post-Fair goals, it was also motivated by his desire that the new Fair contain endless variety. To Bunshaft and the others who called for the Fair to make a single statement and speak with one distinctive voice, Moses replied: *I get a little weary of the avant garde critics who see in a World's Fair only an opportunity to advance their latest ideas, to establish a new school of American planning, architecture and art and place their individual seal on one grand, unified, integrated concept which will astonish the visitor from the hinterland and rock the outer world. . . . The Fair administration belongs to no architectural clique, subscribes to no esthetic creed, favors no period or school and worships at no artistic shrine.* [10]

Rather than proposing a single idea, the Fair aimed, in Moses's words, "to be universal, to have something for everyone." Ostensibly, the Fair was united around the theme "Peace Through Understanding," originally concocted by Jerome Weinstein, a member of the World's Fair Corporation, during the brief period when it was run by Robert Koppel. While Moses accepted the theme, he was quick to add others. In bold letters on the title page of the progress reports issued by the Fair Corporation, the following statement reflected the diversified goals that Moses set out for the new Fair: *The basic purpose of the Fair is Peace through Understanding, that is education of the peoples of the world as to the interdependence of nations to insure a lasting peace. The Fair is dedicated to Man's achievements on a shrinking globe in an expanding universe, his inventions, discoveries, arts, skills and aspirations, to the celebration of the 300th anniversary of the founding of the City of New York, to the opening of Lincoln Center for the Performing Arts, to wholesome entertainment, to the realization of the Metropolitan arterial program, and the completion of Flushing Meadow Park with a legacy of permanent recreational facilities after the Fair.* [11]

The visual theme center for Moses's Fair was the Unisphere, a 140-foot-high, 900,000-pound steel armillary

Left, top and bottom: Trylon and Perisphere, theme center of the 1939/40 Fair. Designed by Harrison & Fouilhoux, the structure was 700 feet high and 200 feet in diameter. Photographs by Bob Golby, collection of The Queens Museum.

sphere covered with the representations of the continents and encircled by three giant rings denoting the first manmade satellites that had recently launched the space age. The emblematic Unisphere was to serve the 1964/65 Fair as the Trylon and Perisphere had served its 1939 predecessor—as the centerpiece of the fairgrounds and as a visual logo for Fair publicity. Occupying the central spot in Flushing Meadow Park, where the Trylon and Perisphere once stood, the Unisphere was the creation of Gilmore Clarke, a longtime Moses collaborator on the Flushing Meadow Park ground plan and the 1939 Fair.

The Unisphere's history was not without incident. One of Moses's first and most difficult tasks on assuming control of the Fair Corporation had been to come up with a visual logo to rival the highly successful Trylon and Perisphere. At first he hoped for an appropriate plan from the design committee, which included both Wallace Harrison and Henry Dreyfuss, the architect and the designer who had created the Trylon and Perisphere and its interior exhibit, "Democracity." When the design committee endorsed Bunshaft's expensive donut-shaped pavilion, Moses turned to Walter Dorwin Teague, the noted industrial designer who had served on the design committee of 1939, to submit a theme center idea. Moses's views on an appropriate central symbol are set forth in an August 21, 1960 memo to his assistant, Stuart Constable:

It gets down to these alternatives.

A. *Pure abstraction. Absolutely nothing doing. Toss it out.*

B. *Understandable abstraction symbolizing theme, with some significance or meaning for the average person.*

C. *U.N. buildings. Kind of corny. Unoriginal. U.N. probably won't like it. Neither will some of our people, but it's not impossible.*

D. *Something from electronic or invention world.*

E. *Throgs Neck or Narrows suspension bridge.*

F. *Onward and upward symbol—Heaven knows what.*

G. *Something else.* [12]

Right: John C. Wenrich, *Rendering of the Unisphere and Rocket Thrower,* 1962, watercolor on paper, 22 × 32¼ in. Collection of Clarke + Rapuano, Inc. Photograph by Jim Strong.

Opposite, top right: Hugh Ferriss, *Drawing of the Unisphere,* 1961, pencil on paper. Photograph courtesy of the Rare Books and Manuscripts Division, New York Public Library, Astor, Lenox, and Tilden Foundations.

Below and opposite, bottom: Construction of the Unisphere, the theme center of the 1964/65 Fair, designed by Gilmore D. Clarke. Photograph courtesy of the Rare Books and Manuscripts Division, New York Public Library, Astor, Lenox, and Tilden Foundations.

Teague's proposal, "Journey to the Stars," was for a 170-foot-high steel and aluminum spiral with helium-filled star-shaped balloons floating above. The spiral was animated by moving lights. In its most ambitious stage, a ride took people to the top.[13] A related two-dimensional design was temporarily used as the Fair logo, but in an August 12, 1960 letter to Gilmore Clarke, Moses expressed his disappointment with Teague's concept. "At the risk of being put down as a barbarian, I think it is a cross between a part of a make and break engine and a bed spring, or should I say between a Malayan Tapir and a window shutter."[14] Another proposal Moses rejected was "The Galaxon," designed by Paul Rudolph, an innovative young architect and dean of the Yale University Department of Architecture. The 160-foot-high, 340-foot in diameter, saucer-shaped concrete structure, sponsored by Portland Cement, featured stations for star viewing, and was tilted at an 18-degree angle to offer an optimum view of the heavens.[15]

Like the Teague and Rudolph proposals, Clarke's giant globe, encircled by rings, celebrated the space age that had begun with the Russian launching of Sputnik in 1957 and continued in America after John F. Kennedy's election as President in 1960. The Unisphere was clearly the type of "understandable" structure "with some significance or meaning for the average person" that Moses had favored in his theme center memorandum. As the world's largest global structure, the Unisphere also appealed to Moses's love of gargantuan scale. Since building the structure required the aid of newly invented high-speed computers to work out complicated technological problems, it also appealed to the engineer in him.[16]

The Unisphere was to be the centerpiece of a group of sculptures that would permanently adorn Flushing

Below: Logo by Walter Dorwin Teague Associates. This design was used by the Fair Corporation in 1961 and later replaced with the official Fair symbol of the Unisphere. Photograph by Phyllis Bilick, collection of The Queens Museum.

Opposite: "Journey to the Stars," proposal for theme center designed by Walter Dorwin Teague Associates. This model was for a 170-foot-high steel and aluminum spiral. Moses rejected the concept. Photograph courtesy of Walter Dorwin Teague Associates.

NEW YORK WORLD'S FAIR 1964-1965

MAN'S ACHIEVEMENTS IN AN EXPANDING UNIVERSE

Opposite: Rendering of "The Galaxon," a proposed theme center designed by architect Paul Rudolph. This concept was refused by Moses who opted for the more "understandable" structure of the Unisphere. Photograph courtesy of Paul Rudolph.

Below, top and bottom: Model of "The Galaxon." The proposed structure was to rise 160 feet. Photographs by Joe A. Watson, courtesy of Paul Rudolph.

Meadow Park. While Moses convinced U.S. Steel to pick up the $2 million bill for its construction (in exchange for the publicity potential), the other sculptures were paid for by the Fair Corporation. Together with the Unisphere, these pieces—*The Rocket Thrower* by Donald De Lue, *Forms in Space* by Theodore Roszak, and Paul Manship's *Celestial Sphere*—were part of a coherent program that celebrated the dawn of the space age. Because each of the pieces required Moses's personal approval, the sculpture chosen clearly reflected a conservative taste in art that had been formed during the 1930s.

Moses was also interested in the Hall of Science that he convinced the city to construct for the Fair. It would be retained as a permanent Museum of Science and Technology in the post-Fair park. His own interest in technology accorded well with the science vogue that swept America in the 1960s. During the Fair, the Hall of Science contained exhibits on space flight, atomic energy, and advances in medicine that had been solicited from government agencies. Its highlight was a large outdoor rocket and spacecraft display provided by NASA.[17] The impressive futuristic building was designed by Wallace Harrison.

For the New York City pavilion, which Moses had built in 1939, he persuaded the city to construct the ambitious "Panorama of the City of New York," a 9,000-square-foot scale model showing all 830,000 buildings in the five-borough metropolis. Designed by Lester Associates, a modelmaking firm often used by Moses, the Panorama duplicated the city with remarkable exactitude. Given that it also celebrated the 300th anniversary of New York City, the 1964 pavilion was particularly lavish. Visitors first saw a model of New York as it was in 1660 (also created by Lester and now at the Museum of the City of New York), then took a "simulated helicopter"

Opposite: Hall of Science designed by Harrison and Abramovitz. Moses convinced the city to construct this building with the intention that it would remain in Flushing Meadow Park as a museum of science and technology. Photograph by Peter Austin Leavens.

Below: Panorama of the City of New York, designed by Lester Associates. This 9,000 square foot model accurately depicted ever, structure in the five boroughs. It was the featured exhibit in the New York City pavilion. Visitors boarded cars for a simulated helicopter ride around New York. The Panorama remains a permanent feature of The Queens Museum. Collection of The Queens Museum. Photograph by Dan Cornish, courtesy of Esto Photographics Inc.

amusement car ride around the edge of the Panorama, accompanied by a taped narration by radio news commentator Lowell Thomas. Then the world's largest model, the Panorama took nearly four years to construct and cost over $900,000.[18] It was not only a successful Fair attraction, but more importantly for Moses, it enjoys a long post-Fair life at the Queens Museum as an educational tool and a masterpiece of modelmaking.

During his long career as a builder, Moses had often commissioned ambitious models to illustrate various projects. His love of models was an aesthetic taste that accorded well with the traditions of world's fairs. Soon after joining the Fair Corporation, Moses commissioned from Lester Associates a large model of the Fairgrounds, ceremoniously used to show visiting dignitaries how the Fair was developing with each new pavilion design. Smaller models, each protectively enclosed under a plastic dome, circulated around the country to promote ticket sales. The Triborough Bridge and Tunnel display at the New York City pavilion featured Lester models of Moses's bridges and tunnels. The New York Power Authority display at the New York State pavilion included Lester's large model of the Robert Moses Dam planned for the St. Lawrence River.

Moses's aesthetic would make its clearest mark on the 1964/65 Fair in those features that would remain permanently in Flushing Meadow Park. But because he was President of the World's Fair Corporation, the person who recruited the Fair's participants and communicated to them about other exhibits, his taste could be perceived throughout the 1964/65 Fair. At the New

Model of the Fair commissioned by Moses and designed by Lester Associates. Photograph courtesy of the Rare Books and Manuscripts Division, New York Public Libary, Astor, Lenox, and Tilden Foundations.

York State pavilion, the architect Philip Johnson (selected by Governor Rockefeller) included a giant floor mosaic showing the Texaco roadmap of the state. It was the world's largest two-dimensional map, a fitting complement for the largest globe and the largest scale model of a city that Moses provided for the Fair.

That Moses had long-standing relations with corporations and other powerful entities was reflected in his choice of Fair participants. The veteran road builder attracted an especially strong transportation zone to the Fair, with ambitious pavilions by General Motors, Ford, and Chrysler. Moses's cordial relations with the Catholic Archdiocese of New York paid off with a large Vatican pavilion highlighted by the display of Michaelangelo's *Pietà*. His love of mainstream popular entertainment led to his personal recruitment of Walt Disney, who made major displays in four pavilions. Moses also affected what was *not* at the Fair. The builder of Jones Beach, long opposed to the bawdy boardwalk atmosphere that cheapened other seasides, was determined that the Fair amusement zone have none of the nudie shows that had been so popular at the 1939/40 Fair.

The Fair, which was a giant public relations effort on behalf of the city, seemed exempt from press criticism at first. As time passed, however, Moses's handling of the enterprise increasingly came under attack. The Moses emphasis on corporate pavilions and popular entertainment particularly repelled New York's intellectuals. This was perhaps an inevitable conflict, rooted in Moses's basic beliefs about what a world's fair was about and what the role of culture should be in such matters.

In a 1938 article he wrote for the *Saturday Evening Post*, Moses had earlier articulated attitudes that were certain to be offensive to Americans who cared deeply about culture:

Below: Floor mosaic, New York State pavilion. The giant Texaco map of New York State was the world's largest two-dimensional map, measuring 144 square feet. Photograph by Gert Berliner.

The early Fairs were glorified markets to which people came to show their wares, to barter and to trade. Amusements were a natural addition, a pleasant relief from the main business and an excuse for bringing the family along. Finally somebody introduced the idea of culture, and then the real fun began. Ever since, there has been an irrepressible conflict among three sets of people—those who are for business first; those who are for attracting people to the site and city by means of amusement and ballyhoo; and, finally, those who see in the fair an opportunity to spread the gospel of beauty and enhance what they call the amenities of civilization. . . . There may be no public announcement of it, but the shows, the entertainments, the amusements, fun, food, drinks, and everything else that goes with a gigantic circus, are going to come out first. . . . Business will run a close second. Culture, which is somehow associated with long walks and aching feet, will be third.[19]

Coinciding with the rise of new political, social, and cultural attitudes in America, the 1964/65 Fair became a lightning rod for attacks by a new generation of thinkers who were increasingly questioning inherited values. More than most, the seventy-year-old Moses represented prewar attitudes; not surprisingly, the Fair he created, with the help of many other elderly men and women who had worked on the 1939/40 Fair, tended to reflect the values of the 1930s. While the patriotic platitudes, consumer dreams, and escapist entertainment of the Depression had played well in 1939, in the affluent 1960s they had hollow appeal to the forward-looking. Typical was the reaction of Vincent J. Scully, Jr., writing for *Life*:

[The Ford Pavilion] is by Disney, who so vulgarizes everything he touches that facts lose all force, living things their stature, and the "history of the world" its meaning. Disney caters to the kind of phony reality—most horribly exemplified by the moving-and-talking figure of Lincoln elsewhere in the Fair—that we all too readily accept in place of the true. Mr. Disney, I'm afraid has our number. But so does Mr. Moses; for when all is said and done, his Fair is exactly the kind of world we are building all over the U.S. right now . . . the Fair is nothing but the concentrated essence of motel, gas station, shopping center and suburb. Why go to New York to find it, then, when we have it all at home?[20]

Never one to take criticism quietly, Moses lashed back in a pamphlet entitled *The Fair, the City, and the Critics*, published by the Fair Corporation at the close of the 1964 season. "Today avant-garde critics and leftwing commentators, traditionally pledged to free speech and respect for opinions of others however distasteful, break all records for intolerance of those who differ with them, especially middle roaders." Moses believed that "jaded publishers," instead of giving "the avant garde a free rein," should "look at the cheerful, eager, polite faces in the crowds at the Fair, the folks in slacks and those in their best bibs and tuckers. . . . That's the Fair. That's New York after three hundred years. That's America."[21]

Moses's strong reaction to criticism of the Fair not only reflected his own argumentative personality, but also the increasing realization that the Fair was facing serious financial problems. Initial estimates had predicted that it would attract 70 million people over its two seasons, but as the 1964 season ended, projections showed that attendance would run about 25 percent below that. This meant a $10 million deficit, a bitter pill for Moses to swallow since he had so emphasized running the Fair as an economic venture. He was quick to blame the press. "All of our studies indicate beyond question that a small but influential segment of the local press, including some magazines of wide circulation which have their headquarters in this city, have been a serious handicap."[22]

So it was that the 1964/65 Fair did not turn out to be the triumphal end of his career that Moses had hoped for when he took over the presidency of the Fair Corporation. But according to Harold Blake, his executive assistant during the Fair years, Moses never considered the Fair the flop his critics have labeled it.[23] Fifty-one million people attended the Fair, a new record for international expositions, and many critics and fairgoers gave the grandiose spectacle unqualified praise. While the Fair did not generate the

monies to pay back notes and to finish Flushing Meadow Park in ambitious style, Moses could point to real accomplishments. The Fair pumped billions into New York's economy and funded numerous lasting improvements to the city's infrastructure. When Flushing Meadow reopened as a city park in 1967, it had come a long way from the mountain of ashes Moses knew from the 1930s. Although a lack of funds prevented the reopening of the water amphitheater, and the New York State pavilion would remain a rotting hulk, a new sports stadium, outdoor concert bowl, science museum, botanical garden, zoo, and a rich collection of park sculpture were added to the boating lake, ice-skating rink, open fields, walkways, and fountains created in conjunction with the 1939/40 Fair. Flushing Meadow Park is today the crowning jewel of the parks Moses created for New York City.

The remarkable final surge of Fair attendance, with 7 million people attending during the final three weeks, perhaps proved that Moses's Fair was a fine show after all.[24] Now, twenty-five years later, the 1964/65 Fair, like the 1939/40 Fair, can be fondly remembered. More importantly, it can be seen in its proper perspective: as a direct outgrowth of the earlier Fair and a grand showcase of the dynamic changes, both good and bad, that took place between the 1930s and the 1960s.

Above: Rendering of the post-Fair park, 1966, designed by Andrews & Clark, Inc., and Clarke + Rapuano, Inc. Photograph courtesy of the Triborough Bridge and Tunnel Authority.

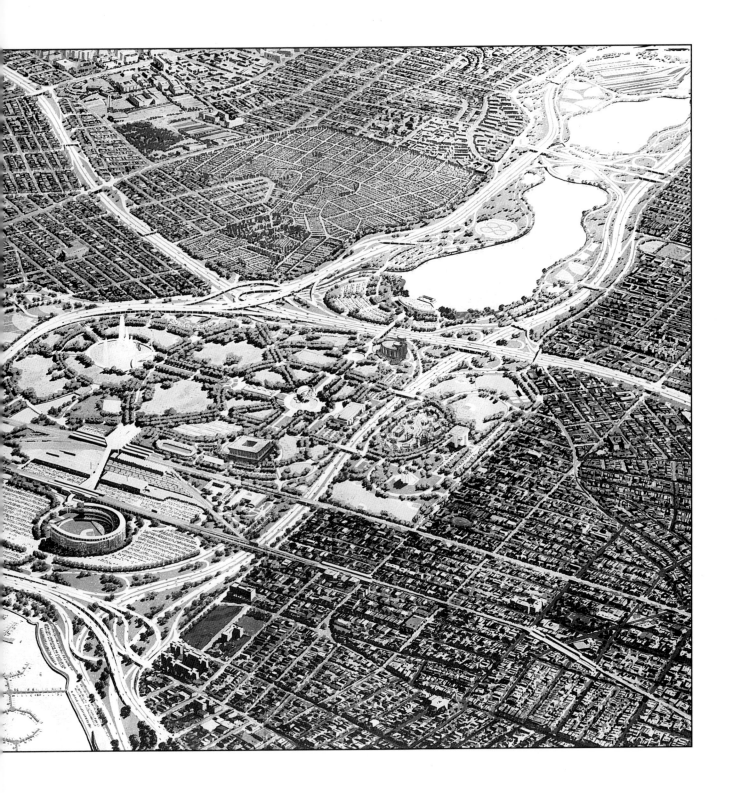

Above: Rendering of
"Journey to the Stars"
theme center proposal by
Walter Dorwin Teague
Associates. Photograph
courtesy of Walter Dorwin
Teague Associates.

New Frontiers: *Science and Technology at the Fair*

Sheldon J. Reaven

"Progress" has poisoned the atmosphere, polluted the rivers and lakes, depleted the forests and hatched a whole new set of problems that threaten our environment. If we don't get some balance in our environment soon, life on this planet, as we know it, is finished.

Nothing shows how widely held these sentiments are so much as the fact that none other than Ann Landers has seen fit to voice them.[1] Fears about the course of science and technology, and about man's ability to guide them wisely and humanely, are no longer shrugged off as the exaggerations of professors or activists. While popular fascination with many products of science and technology—the VCR, the Space Shuttle—continues, the unbridled love affair is over, the marriage shaky.

This state of affairs could not be further from the confident world of the early sixties. John F. Kennedy began his presidency in 1961, declaring, "We stand today at the edge of a New Frontier: the frontier of the 1960s." America also stood at the very crest of its postwar technological and economic prowess. By 1964 Americans were spellbound by the space program (and committed to landing on the moon), vigorously pursuing a nuclear power program to provide electricity "too cheap to meter," and crossing the threshold of the computer and information era.

This spirit of promise, of large undertaking, was conveyed in the 1964/65 New York World's Fair. Its themes "Man's Achievements in an Expanding Universe" and "A Millenium of Progress" celebrated the boundless potential of science and technology for human betterment. The themes "Peace through Understanding" and "It's a Small World" embodied (as did Kennedy's Peace Corps) a belief that technology, knowledge, and communication would inexorably bring people ever closer together. ("Peace through Understanding" is often recalled as *the* Fair theme, but the wording, relative priority, and degree of formal sanction of the themes shifted in official and semi-official Fair literature.)

That such confidence should mark a world's fair built by a generation that defeated Hitler, laid down interstate highways, conquered polio, and so on, is not surprising. Yet the contrast with today's diminished expectations is even more striking when one recalls that the 1939/40 New York World's Fair, too, declared its faith in new technology, democratically planned for the benefit of the common man—indeed, more thoughtfully and self-consciously so than did the 1964/65 Fair. The 1939/40 Fair was a daring, captivating, even defiant beacon of hope in the face of the gathering world cataclysm and the lingering Depression.

When one examines the 1964/65 Fair, the recurring reaction is that the times were, so to speak, "pre"—pre-Challenger, pre-Chernobyl, pre-Bhopal, pre-Vietnam War, not to mention the

November 1965 Northeast blackout, the counterculture of the later 1960s, the pill, Japanese cars, Watergate, Pac-Man and the PC, acid rain, Love Canal, the oil embargo and energy crisis, the greenhouse effect, the "postindustrial" economy, Three Mile Island, and the garbage barge. These developments have profoundly affected the outlook for many of the technologies displayed at the Fair. However, every period has its symbolic disasters and landmark events, including environmental and technological ones (*Titanic, Hindenburg,* Dust Bowl, Hiroshima). The interesting question is why the ones since 1964 did, and the ones before 1964 did not, so profoundly shape what the nation and the world think about the benefits, costs, and risks of technology, about whether it is a servant or a master.

The New Technological Frontiers
The Space Age

Neil Armstrong stepped onto the lunar surface in 1969, a mere eight years after Alan Shepard entered space for fifteen minutes in a cramped Mercury space capsule. The 1964/65 Fair arrived right in the middle of those matchless dawn years of feverish activity and glory in outer space. During the Fair itself, Ed White took the first "space walk" tethered to Gemini 4, Ranger 7 careened into the lunar surface, sending pictures a thousand times more detailed than the best photos taken from earth, and millions of people, following schedules published in daily papers, watched nightly for Echo 2, the new, 135-foot aluminum-coated passive communications satellite visible to the naked eye. During these years nearly every mission got saturation television coverage, from liftoff to splashdown, as each new technology, piece of equipment, or astronaut skill required for the moon program was tested in turn.

America's infatuation with space was reflected, and concentrated, in the

U.S. Space Park sponsored by NASA and the U.S. Department of Defense. Displayed were: Project Mercury spacecraft; Gemini two-man spacecraft; model of Apollo spacecraft; lunar excursion vehicle; lower portion of the Saturn V moon rocket; X-15 rocket-powered research airplane; and Thor-Delta, Atlas and Titan II rockets. Photograph by Peter Austin Leavens.

Fair. First, the instrumentalities and paraphernalia of space exploration were everywhere. A mighty array of rockets loomed in the two-acre United States Space Park sponsored by NASA, the Defense Department, and the Fair itself. The Park's exhibits included a full-scale model of the lower propulsion section of the colossal Saturn V "moon rocket," a Titan II booster with its two-man Gemini capsule, and an Atlas with its Mercury. At ground level, one could inspect the Mercury flown on the second American manned orbital flight and full-scale models of the three-man Apollo Command and Service modules, the sacramental Lunar Excursion Model, and Gemini spacecraft. Unmanned spacecraft shown included real or replica lunar Rangers and Surveyors, a Mariner II Venus probe, Tiros and Nimbus weather satellites, Syncom, Telstar, Relay, and Echo communications satellites, and Explorer and Discoverer research satellites.

The Federal pavilion included displays on the phases of the manned space program, the use of satellites for detecting weapons, and the 1962 Mariner mission to Venus. Chrysler had its own ten-story rocket. Diverse state and national pavilions mounted exhibits on communications satellites, space capsules, space history, the search for intelligent extraterrestrial life, and a research rocket that gave the visitor a sense of motion. The pavilions of many major industries and companies included material on the sponsor's contributions to space science and technology. For example, the Avenue of Progress (part of the GM pavilion) included a "Space Age Research" theme center featuring a solar space mirror, an articulated lunar vehicle, the world's largest cosmic-ray spark chamber, and exhibits on space navigation technologies. And Kodak built an artificial lunar landscape as a backdrop for snapshots.

The great Unisphere (once to have been called "Earth and Orbits"), with its

Below, top: Arrival of Thor-Delta rocket at U.S. Space Park. Photograph courtesy of the Rare Books and Manuscripts Division, New York Public Library, Astor, Lenox, and Tilden Foundations.

Below, bottom: Cosmic ray spark chamber exhibited in the General Motors pavilion. Photograph courtesy of the Rare Books and and Manuscripts Division, New York Public Library, Astor, Lenox, and Tilden Foundations.

Opposite: Lunar landscape roof of the Eastman Kodak pavilion designed by Kahn & Jacobs. It was created as a backdrop for snapshots. Photograph courtesy of Photofest.

three satellite orbit rings, symbolized the human emergence into space, as did the surrounding sculptures *The Rocket Thrower*, and *Forms in Space*. Viewed from the edge of the pool, the Unisphere has the dimensions Earth would have if viewed from a height of six thousand miles.

Secondly, space fever manifested itself at the Fair in the form of several multi-media simulated journeys into space. Next to the Space Park, in the Hall of Science, 400 visitors at a time could see two full-sized vehicles—precursors of the Shuttle and Skylab—"Rendezvous in Space" high overhead as part of an engulfing multi-media show sponsored by the Martin-Marietta Company. Inside the 96-foot-diameter Moon Dome, named for its exterior plastic lunar relief map, in the Transportation and Travel pavilion, audiences were encircled by a screen which led them, via Cinerama, "To the Moon and Beyond": "YOU will be propelled on the most fantastic, incredible voyage through billions of miles of space . . . from its utmost outer reaches . . . back to Earth itself, and into the center of the minutest atom." Ford's "Magic Skyway" ride, "Into the Space Age," the Federal pavilion ride, "The Past as Prologue," and the GM "Futurama" ride also made spectacular "stops" in space.

By most accounts, the public generally took time to read the captions and texts for exhibits on space subjects. Why was interest so high? To begin with, space exploration was *utterly* new (the 1939/40 Fair had anticipated the atomic age but not the space age). The pictures of earth from orbit offered a global political and ecological perspective on humanity's troubles. Moreover, space exploration was looked upon as noble (offering knowledge and the satisfaction of curiosity) and heroic (requiring bravery and adventure). Space represented an unsullied arena where human venality and conflict might remain unknown. The sheer

Below, top: Model of a space taxi, from the "Journey into Space" exhibit in the Hall of Science pavilion. Photograph courtesy of Peter M. Warner.

Below, bottom: Model of orbiting space laboratory, from the "Journey into Space" exhibit. A brief show simulated a trip into space with the use of motion pictures and sound effects. Photograph courtesy of Peter M. Warner.

Opposite: Interior of the Great Hall, Hall of Science pavilion, showing "Journey into Space," an exhibit presented by the Martin-Marietta Corporation. Photograph by Peter Austin Leavens.

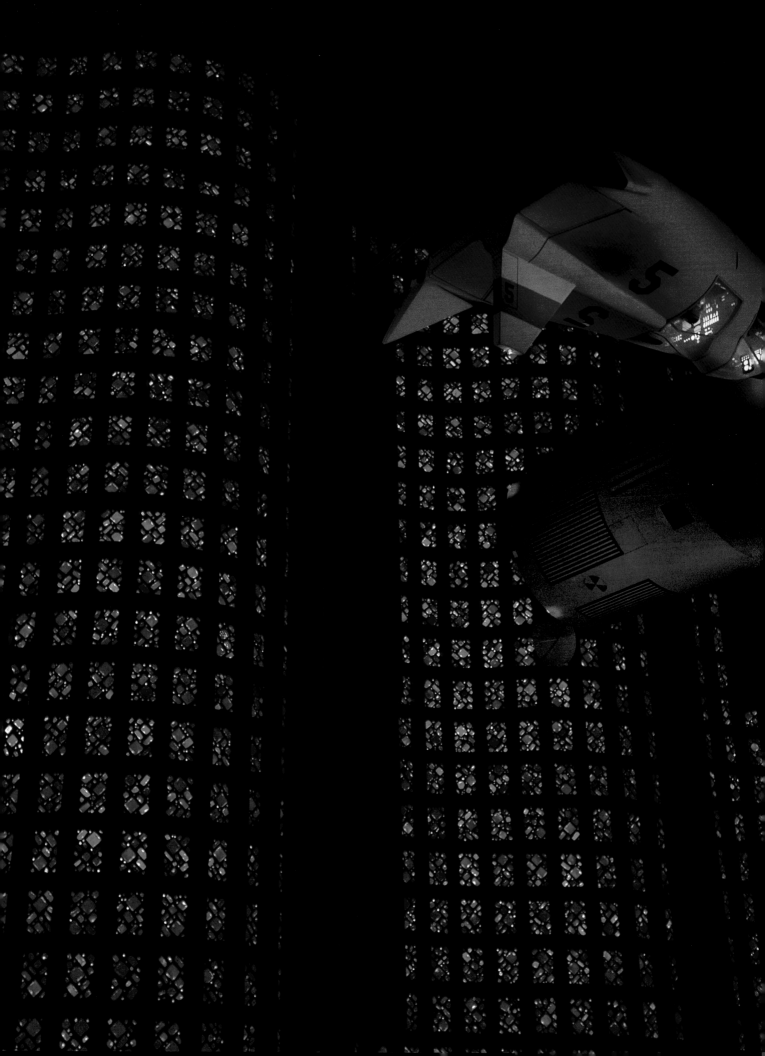

scale and power of the equipment were awesome. Interest also was sustained by the constant risk of failure during the march to the moon, as in the later Apollo 1 fire, which killed three astronauts, and the Apollo 13 space emergency. There is, finally, the elemental pull the wonders of the heavens have always exercised on the human mind.

The years since the Fair, especially since the last lunar expedition in December 1972, may have clouded the picture. Space nuclear weapons and battle tactics have been under development. On the other hand, space satellites are the *sine qua non* of arms treaty verification; debate continues as to what research and manufacture should be permitted in space; issues of space law and territoriality are not settled; NASA is concerned about the litter and waste disposal problems of potential lunar settlements. Familiarity may have dimmed the enthusiasm of some people. Arguments continue as to whether large space programs are worth the money and resources they consume, in light of pressing problems on earth.

Still, mankind has, since the Apollo program, dwelled in space, and, with instruments, seen the rings of Saturn, Martian sunsets, volcanoes on Io, the Jovian Great Red Spot, and many other strange sights. Space is turning out to be far more varied and interesting than anyone had imagined.

The fascination with space remains: Washington's National Air and Space Museum, where crowds still queue up to disbelievingly touch a few small moon rocks, is one of the world's most visited museums. But the World's Fair of 1964/65 was the first such "museum" on earth, and brought home the message that "in this Age of Space, not even the sky will be the limit."[2]

The Information Age: Computers and Communication

An observer for *Holiday* magazine

Below, top: Moon dome of the Transportation and Travel pavilion designed by Clive Entwistle Associates. This 96-foot-high structure presented an accurate relief map of the moon. Photograph courtesy of Peter M. Warner

Below, bottom: Workmen repair the roof's lunar surface. Photograph courtesy of the Rare Books and Manuscripts Division, New York Public Library, Astor, Lenox, and Tilden Foundations.

Opposite, top left: Two-Man Space Station Simulation exhibit in the General Electric pavilion. Photograph courtesy of the Rare Books and Manuscripts Division, New York Public Library, Astor, Lenox, and Tilden Foundations.

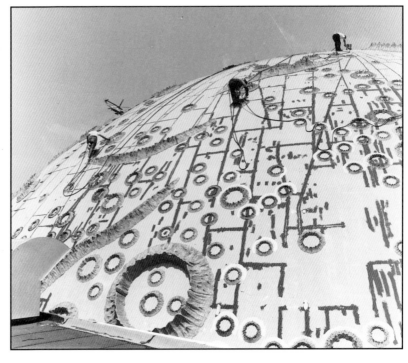

Below, top: Astronaut Gordon Cooper receiving an honorary plaque at the U.S. Space Park. Photograph courtesy of the Rare Books and Manuscripts Division, New York Public Library, Astor, Lenox, and Tilden Foundations.

Below, bottom: Kolonel Keds, "The Rocket Man," flew around the Unisphere via rocket belt. His sponsor was U.S. Rubber, maker of Keds sneakers. Photograph courtesy of the Rare Books and Manuscripts Division, New York Public Library, Astor, Lenox, and Tilden Foundations.

warned that the 1964/65 Fair depicted "a world computerized to the teeth, a push-button world purveying instant fact and instant wisdom. It is a world proud of its systems of swift communication, sure of its lightning answers."[3] At the National Cash Register pavilion, on request, a computer printed out lists: famous events that took place on February 17; the essential sights of Rome. At the Better Living Center, computers generated lists of colors to use in home decorating; at the Parker Pen pavilion, a computer met requests for pen pals in cities all over the globe by picking names from its stored directory. Clairol, the Protestant Center, General Electric, the Hall of Free Enterprise, the Hall of Education, and other pavilions offered similar diversions in which computers instantly shuffled stored information. Unfortunately, some of these presentations gave the impression that the computer in question was engaging in something like thinking.

The IBM pavilion was something else again. It represented a major effort to *teach* the principles of probability (there was a giant quincunx), logical structure, and abstraction, to explain how their material embodiments (for example, computer circuits and memory cores) work, and to persuade people that computers were beneficial and, in a later phrase, "user-friendly." A puppet theater argued that complex problems, language learning, shape recognition, and intelligence itself could ultimately be reduced to the "yes/no" structure of a game of Twenty Questions, only much longer.

The same claim was advanced in IBM exhibits that used a computer for very limited tasks in translation (Russian to English) and pattern recognition (handwritten characters). The computer (actually ninety miles away) was easy to fool and often made mistakes. Despite the breathtaking leaps in computer power and organization since the Fair, the

Below: Women could peer into special mirrors to see how they looked with a variety of hairdos at the Clairol Color Carousel. Photograph courtesy of the Rare Books and Manuscripts Division, New York Public Library, Astor, Lenox, and Tilden Foundations.

Below left, top and bottom: IBM's Computers at Work display designed by Charles and Ray Eames. Computers demonstrated how data written in Russian was easily and quickly translated into English. Visitors were asked to choose any date within 100 years. The computer system could deliver a printed card detailing significant historical events that occurred on the date. Photographs by Cornell Capa, courtesy of Cornell Capa/Magnum Photos, Inc.

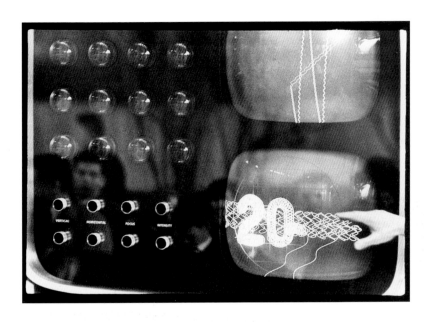

Below: Night view of the
IBM pavilion designed by
Eero Saarinen. Photograph
by Bob Golby, collection
of The Queens Museum.

satisfactory performance of such tasks, many of which any five-year-old child can perform, has continued to elude successive waves of "artificial intelligence" researchers and theorists. It remains an open question whether most intelligent processes can be reduced to structures amenable to digital computers.

The *Holiday* observer also remarked that, "IBM knows very well it can't sell or rent a computer to me, and most likely not to you, either."[4] This truism of the day underscores the strides taken since the era of the clumsy early mainframe computers. No one paid much attention to the computer in the Japanese pavilion either (a Fujitsu FACOM); it printed out itineraries for travelers— more lists.

The most wonderful feature of the IBM pavilion was its giant, ninety-foot-high ellipsoidal theater, called the "Information Machine." A twelve-tier "People Wall" moved five hundred people up inside the theater. A fifteen-minute cinema creation by Charles Eames, with music by Elmer Bernstein, using fourteen synchronized projectors and nine screens inside the egg, cleverly discussed the operation of the brain and the computer.

The National Cash Register pavilion also provided thoughtful exhibits, with displays on the history of counting devices, the sea of paperwork in modern society, and a fully automated branch-bank system. In a similar vein, the General Motors pavilion envisioned a punchcard-operated Delco "auto service center of the future."

Several new communications technologies were displayed and used at the Fair. The Bell System pavilion introduced the Picturephone, using the device to interview fairgoers about their own reaction to it. Other new or recently perfected Bell technologies included the Vocoder, touch-tone phones, undersea cables with time-shared voice transmission, and the laser and maser.

Visitors also could make voiceprints and view the workings of transistors and of the entire Bell communications network. Upstairs, a fifteen-minute ride led the viewer on a tour of the history of communications "From Drumbeat to Telstar"; the first transatlantic satellite television broadcast had come, via Telstar, only in 1962.

At RCA, one could watch an operating color television studio that was hooked up to more than 250 color sets around the fairgrounds. This system was used for televising announcements, ceremonies, and pictures of lost children.

The information exhibits advanced two broad themes: that rapid, globalized communications would break down barriers of misunderstanding and draw people together, and that the products of the information age (including automation) would save much time and labor. The use of the media by Mikhail Gorbachev or Pope John Paul II exemplifies the first claim, and the use of the word processors the second. Yet there may also be danger in spending too much time "communicating" by machine: listening to Walkmen, playing computer games, and using call-in telephone services. Perhaps, the "information revolution" is raising barriers between people passively isolated in media "cocoons." "Dialogue," in some instances, has sharpened, not reduced international rivalry: peace doesn't always come through understanding.

Against the claim that the then touted products of the information age saved time and labor, it may be said that people in the 1980s appear more pressed and stressed for time than ever. Furthermore, the immense data manipulation capacity of computers has led to the indiscriminate recording of more and more useless data. And the use of paper has soared, a development for which another product of the information age, the copying machine, must share responsibility.

Below, top left: Family communicating via picturephone at the Bell System pavilion. Photograph courtesy of AT&T Archives and the Rare Books and Manuscripts Division, New York Public Library, Astor, Lenox, and Tilden Foundation.

Below, bottom left: Demonstration of the Bell System's Vocoder, a visual speech device that transformed voices into visual symbols on a television screen. Photograph courtesy of AT&T Archives and Peter M. Warner.

Below, top right: Exterior of the RCA pavilion designed by Malcolm B. Wells. The pavilion housed the Fair's "Official Color Television Communication Center" which broadcasted news, announcements and ceremonies on 250 color television sets placed throughout the fairgrounds. Photograph courtesy of Peter M. Warner.

Below, bottom right: Visitors could see themselves on television in the closed-circuit display at the RCA pavilion. Photograph courtesy of the New York Daily News.

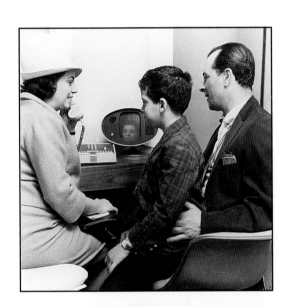

The Atomic Age: Electricity Too Cheap to Meter

For the 1964/65 Fair, the atomic age meant one thing: nuclear power. A flood of energy from fission and fusion reactors would run ever more electrified homes and in time lift humanity's standard of living to utopian levels by powering the gargantuan macro-engineering schemes heralded in "Futurama" and other venues. This message dwarfed the small attention given to atomic weapons and radiation exposure issues: although memories of the Cuban Missile Crisis, milk contaminated with strontium-90 from fallout, and the treaty banning atmospheric atomic tests were fresh, people do not come to a fair to be reminded of the nuclear war albatross.

The "must-see" GE Progressland pavilion, which a *New York Times* reviewer said deserved the "prize for the most grandiose science exhibit for its fusion display," pulled no punches in getting across its main theme, "Peace through Understanding; Progress through Electric Power," and its subsidiary theme, "The Wonders of Atomic Energy." A moving ramp first carried one upstairs to a moving theater, the Carousel of Progress, which swung past Disney "Audio-Animatronic" dramatizations of the benefits electricity conferred on American homes of different eras. A moving Time Tube and a Disney-designed Corridor of Mirrors then brought one to the Skydome Spectacular to experience electricity's future—helped by a phalanx of eighty-seven coordinated projectors using the curved expanse of the pavilion dome's interior as a screen. At the time, this was the largest screen ever built: eighty feet high, two hundred feet wide. On it one saw—and viscerally felt—the immense power of lightning, storms, and thermonuclear fusion (literally, solar energy).

A little numb, one took a spiral downramp to a large well at the center of Progressland to watch "the creation on earth of a miniature sun, offering a glimpse of the future in which man, a twentieth-century version of Apollo, will harness the sun to his industrial chariot, to provide undreamed of abundance for all mankind everywhere."[5]

A big clear Lexan dome surrounded the apparatus. Inside were two three-foot-long quartz tubes filled with deuterium plasma. Inside them, after a three-minute countdown, a million amperes of current created a magnetic field 200,000 times stronger than earth's. And inside this invisible bottle, for six millionths of a second, millions of the deuterium nuclei fused at a temperature of one hundred million degrees:

During the Fair, the reaction is repeated every six minutes for twelve hours a day, seven days of the week. Those watching see a tremendous flash accompanied with a loud bang, signifying the birth cry of a new age, which, in the course of two decades or so, will open for mankind a source of electrical energy great enough to last for billions of years, with the oceans of the world serving as an inexhaustible reservoir of fuel for a new industrial civilization.[6]

Commercial fission reactors, on the other hand, were already a reality. GE emphasized the rapid expansion of a routine, off-the-shelf product:

. . . atomic power generating stations have become standard items in the General Electric Product Handbook this month . . . [one] can now order either nuclear reactors or complete atomic power plants "by the book" at firm prices for $15 million, less fuel, for a plant rated at 50 megawatts . . . to slightly more than $100 million for a 1 million kilowatt plant.[7]

Some of this electricity would be used in the all-electric GE Medallion Home.

One also learned astounding physics at GE: a gram of electrons would contain 1.1 billion billion billion of them; two grams of protons at opposite poles of the earth would repel one another with a force of twenty-six *tons*.

Exhibits at Ford, Westinghouse, Transportation and Travel, the New York Power Authority, and elsewhere made many of the same points concerning the future of atomic power and the end-uses

of this energy.

The U.S. Atomic Energy Commission (ancestor of both the Nuclear Regulatory Commission and the U.S. Department of Energy) had rejected a Fair proposal to build and operate a mobile nuclear fission plant at the Fair, instead contributing[8] an Atomsville USA exhibit where one could try out remote "hot cell" manipulators for handling radioactive materials and run a simulated reactor. This exhibit, and one sponsored by the U.S. Office of Civil Defense, also discussed the fallout shelter program.

There is no need to dwell on the changed prospects for nuclear power since the Fair: in spite of major scientific advances, commercial fusion has receded into the twenty-first century; Chernobyl, Three Mile Island, and Shoreham symbolize the safety, environmental, and economic roadblocks that have beset the fission industry; the nation's nuclear waste disposal program, a $50 billion project begun in 1982, has foundered. Some theorists argue that electricity, especially when produced by big central power plants, is exactly the wrong form of energy for many tasks. And no one

This page: Appliances designed by Walter Dorwin Teague Associates and displayed in the Festival of Gas pavilion. The Norge Dish Maker (below, left) recycled plastic dishes. Dirty tableware was ground into pellets and re-formed into new dishes. The number of placesettings required was set on the production counter and the machine would mold the plates, saucers, cups and glasses requested. The Norge Refrigerator (below, right) featured a main refrigeration compartment below a circular work surface. The contents were rotated to the door by stepping on a base switch. Garments were placed on hangers and cleaned overnight in The Home Dry Cleaner appliance (top left). Photographs courtesy of Walter Dorwin Teague Associates.

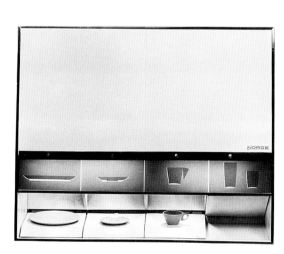

now says that nuclear power is going to be "too cheap to meter" (a phrase coined by Alvin Weinberg in the 1950s).

When viewed today, the Fair's atomic exhibits, however idealistic, however enthralling, bring home the fact that many of the relevant technical challenges were underestimated and sometimes ignored. Social structures for managing these complex technologies across generations are woefully inadequate, and insufficient attention was paid to the cradle-to-grave, "total systems" aspects of these technologies—for example, waste disposal, weapons connections, fuel costs, and contaminated sites. Prospects for nuclear power may revive, if "safe" reactors can be successfully developed, as we face the "greenhouse effect" associated with the continued use of fossil fuels. It remains to be seen if nuclear power is a godsend or Trojan horse.

The Consumer Age: New Materials and Products for Everyday Life

Oh, there's a Great Big Beautiful Tomorrow
Shining at the end of every day
There's a Great Big Beautiful Tomorrow
And tomorrow's just a dream away[9]

Like any proper world's fair, the 1964/65 event was a paradise for shoppers, gadgeteers, and homemakers. New products were triumphantly unveiled, although Bell's Picturephone and Du Pont's Corfam synthetic had nothing like Nylon's impact at the 1939 Fair (it became Du Pont's biggest money-maker ever). Curious contraptions were everywhere. Take the Norge Dish Maker. One of several distinctively futuristic components of the Norge Kitchen designed by the firm of Walter Dorwin Teague for the Festival of Gas pavilion, the Dish Maker ground, washed, and dried the family's plastic dinnerware and molded the pellets into new plates, cups and saucers. Today it might be called a plastic recycler.

Below, top: The Crystal Palace of Fashion in the Better Living Center. Decor was inspired by London's Crystal Palace of 1851. Photograph courtesy of the Rare Books and Manuscripts Division, New York Public Libary, Astor, Lenox, and Tilden Foundations.

Below, bottom: One of fourteen integrated room settings featuring "Futorian" upholstered furniture in the Pavilion of American Interiors. Photograph courtesy of Photofest.

The parade of goods seemed endless. One could visit a Gallery of Kitchens and a Crystal Palace of Fashion in the huge Better Living Center, a Promenade of Interiors, a Formica World's Fair House, "and much, much more."

Many of the new products for home, car, and office, from heart valve to "miracle fabric" to construction material, were made of new plastics and other synthetic polymers. So were large parts of many pavilions themselves. In this respect, as with cars, roads, and airplanes, the 1964/65 Fair delivered on the predictions of 1939; the petroleum-based synthetic revolution led to broad changes in manufacturing technology.

The chemical science and engineering behind these developments were popularized in the Du Pont pavilion. Its "Wonderful World of Chemistry" was a musical, designed by Broadway's Michael Brown, that included numbers like "The Happy Plastics Family." The theater had everything: a Tedlar roof, Delrin doorknobs, Antron and Fabrilite seat fabrics, Dacron fire hoses, Zytel hinges, Mylar stage curtains, and Hylene foam undercarpeting. But the carpets themselves were of venerable Nylon.

Another Du Pont hit was a live, Mr. Wizard-style show called "Chemical Magic," which illustrated the basic physical properties and processes that made the new materials possible: for example, "thixotropic" substances alternately gelled and liquefied, explaining how no-drip paint worked; rubber balls frozen in liquid freon shattered when dropped; liquid, luminescent dyes changed color with each pouring. The visitor's exit was "brightened by a forest of neon lights spelling out some of Du Pont's many products: Neoprene, Zerex, Corfam, Savalux, Zepel, etc."[10]

Exotic materials technologies were explained at GM's Avenue of Progress, the Hall of Science, Ford's own Hall of

Below, top: Du Pont pavilion designed by Voorhees, Walker, Smith, Smith & Haines. Photograph courtesy of Haines, Lundberg, Waehler.

One of the "feats of wizardry through chemistry" in the Du Pont pavilion: demonstration of miraculous no-drip paint. Photograph courtesy of the Rare Books and Manuscripts Division, New York Public Libary, Astor, Lenox, and Tilden Foundations.

Science, and elsewhere. They included thin metallic coatings, metallic ceramics, self-lubricating parts, glass-plastic hybrids, ceramic sponges, thermoelectric devices, and microelectronic, solid state devices. These technologies, especially those involving miniaturization, feedback and control, standardization, and quality control, were critical to the development of computer, spacecraft, and atomic power systems. A number of exhibits were also devoted to biological science topics—especially DNA—in the realm of drugs and personal health.

Many of these exhibits were quite sophisticated, as indicated by this perspective from the designer of the Avenue of Progress: "We figure that maybe one-tenth of one percent of the people who come to the 'Futurama' will be interested in this kind of exhibit. At the same time, we *want* to talk to that one tenth of one percent. The bright high-school youngster who's interested in science."[11] These comments illuminate another mission of the 1964/65 Fair, during the course of which President Lyndon Johnson developed large science education programs to meet the national concern that had been triggered by Sputnik in 1957.

Today two kinds of questions about the Fair's portrayal of consumer and materials technologies would be raised. First, the questions about consumer culture that have been symbolized since the Fair by hippies *and* yuppies are as urgent as ever. Does a "throwaway society" teach the wrong values and squander resources? In the pursuit of Cuisinarts and pasta machines, is recognition of the difference between need and desire blurred? Do all people get a fair share? Might consumer "progress" fragment families and dismember communities? The last "stop" on GE's Carousel of Progress was a programmed, all-electric Gold Medallion Home. The residents told the audience,

Below, top and bottom: Scenes from "Wonderful World of Chemistry" presented in the Du Pont pavilion. This lively musical revue, written and produced by Broadway composer Michael Brown, traced the history of chemistry. Live actors, dressed in Oleg Cassini fashions made of Du Pont fibers, interacted with filmed performers as part of the "amazing" show. Photographs by Bob Golby, collection of The Queens Museum.

with pride, "You're probably wondering what happened to Grandma and Grandpa. Well, they're no longer with us . . . they have their own home now, in a community for senior citizens."[12]

The lack of discussion of environmental issues involving plastics (and the consumption and production of new materials generally) is the second area of concern. Versatile, lightweight, durable, sanitary, noncorroding, waterproof, and cheap to mass produce, plastics have benefited millions. Environmentalists of earlier days (including 1939) praised them precisely for their nondegradability. The degree of environmental harm from plastics and their substitute materials, including "natural" ones, is yet unknown. One answer may be to recycle plastics— perhaps it's time for a second look at the Dish Maker.

Macro-engineering: Integrated Visions of the Technological Future

New technologies were then and still are wondrous, powerful tools . . . for doing what? The 1939 Fair organization, much more so than that of 1964, took care to treat this question thoughtfully and coherently, especially in its theme exhibits,[13] asking *who* has the right to decide the answer and *how,* and distinguishing among what can be done with technological tools, what needs to be done, and what it is morally right to do. But for visitors to both fairs, the one word that said it all about what the technologies were for was "Futurama."

Both GM "Futuramas" imagined a macro-engineered future: one dominated by technological systems on tremendous scales, in terms of energy and materials requirements and yields, as well as sheer physical size and logistical complexity. The transportation, food, energy, raw material, manufacturing, and information systems would provide "a new life of abundance and a greater dignity for us

all."[14]

Seventy-thousand patient people on any given day waited to board one of 463 three-passenger *Fiberglas* cars for a fifteen-minute ride[15] along an 1850-foot track. Accompanied by music by James Fagas and a poetic text by Edward Reveaux and GM staffers dramatically read by Alexander Scourby, they *saw:*

• *a lunar colony with articulated, all-terrain crawlers for expeditions, and then a space station with hovering rockets (with radiation shields);*

• *in Antarctica, an artificial port piercing the ice shelf (thus accessible by submarine) and an underground global weather/climate forecasting center fed data from air, land, sea, and space; ice excavators;*

• *10,000 feet undersea, claw-handed "aquacopters" seeking minerals and ore, and atomic-powered submarines drilling for oil and transporting it to refineries; sea harvesting operations, and an underwater resort (Hotel Atlantis);*

• *a jungle juggernaut, in which, with the use of a laser, a paved road is built "in one continuous operation!" through a jungle;*[16]

• *a computerized, automated desert farming and food processing complex irrigated by desalinated seawater and remotely controlled from a tall, glassy tower, giving on spectacular suburban homes in high mountains; the four-level home has a pool and an automated repair shop for its three cars;*

• *a bargeway and transcontinental highway leading to the city of tomorrow, with its inevitable*[17] *gleaming spires and separate levels for different modes of electronically controlled traffic, including underground freight; there is "ample space for parking."*

General Motors planners worked out these visions in great detail, down to the number and type of crops in the desert, mechanisms of climate control in domes, crew needed for crawlers and "aquacopters," designs for mobile homes for jungle workers, and standard freight container sizes. They assessed demographic and social trends as well as prospects for emerging technologies. No one was surprised when they found that cars, trucks, and roads would fare so well in their future.

Critics and visitors liked the "Futurama" ride, but not all approved of its macro-engineering vision, or of similar ones at the Fair: the City of Tomorrow ("Space City") on Ford's Magic Skyway ride; scenes in "From Space to the Atom"

Below: In the General Motors "Futurama," visitors were shown various environments of the future. This view shows an Antarctic meteorology station located beneath polar ice. Photograph courtesy of General Motors.

at Transportation and Travel; in GE's Skydome Spectacular; and in "A Journey into Space" in the Hall of Science. Peter Lyon, the *Holiday* writer, thought, "It is a city engineered for machines but not designed for people, not for me."[18] Nor was the reviewer for *Industrial Design* pleased:

Throbbing, pulsing, permeating supertorque highways in multiple tubes to everywhere and all devoid of outdoor advertising signs. Whoosh! right through the city and we still have religion (a church building preserved maintains our religious values) . . . This is what really is or darn well will be, but, as in a mirror, and cleaned up, spit and polished, hard edges and interactions removed—no bomb, no homicide, no lust of the kind that is either interesting or forbidden, no peace or war marches . . . GM and Ford assume for tomorrow more of the same and that people will not change essentially, other than to the degree that more *machines and a more machined environment will be an everlasting need.*[19]

What might be said today?

1. Many people continue to advocate macro-projects like those of "Futurama." The L-5 society wants to build space colonies. There is a plan to stop the greenhouse effect by removing vast quantities of carbon from fossil fuel emissions and storing it on the deep ocean floor. And there is a Society for Macro-Engineering. These groups regard the costs of such programs as investments that yield hundredfold returns to society. Counterpoised is an entire school of thought that has grown up since the 1960s: "soft technology" (or "Small Is Beautiful") advocates contend that small-scale, decentralized, locally controllable technologies are generally healthier for people, society, and the ecosystem. They also point out that the upkeep required to keep the large infrastructure operating, and safe, is an Achilles' heel.

The macro-engineers continue to value mobility as both a means and end. Their opposites reply that mobility in our society has, for all its benefits, given rise to rootlessness (serial friendships with successive moves) and shattered rural communities.

2. "Where's the EIS?" The Fair took place five years before passage of the National Environmental Policy Act, which requires environmental impact statements for many construction projects. Few people were thinking about the environment then. GE's three-football-field-long, five-story-high, *atomic-powered* jungle road builder would make one mile of elevated four-lane highway *each hour,* twenty-four hours a day. This would probably be a disaster: in an ongoing crisis that may have global impact, the Brazilians are currently losing their thin soil, and cutting 70,000 acres of Amazon forest *daily,* and their own ambitious road-building program is much to blame for this Pyrrhic conquest. Adverse environmental effects could also come from the 100-foot-long insectiform laser tree clipper that *preceded* the road builder: it sprayed cleared areas with chemicals to retard subsequent growth. The "Futurama" ocean-mining program raises the specter of oil spills and harm to marine life (here it is appropriate to note that whaling ships were present in "Futurama"). The Antarctic and desert farm schemes have their own risks.

3. "Futurama" literature repeatedly refers to the conquest of barren, useless, "waste" land, of making such areas productive, and the like. It is now realized that such lands provide important, often irreplaceable ecological services. The same change in attitude applies to the Fair site itself. It was often disparaged as a swamp, a salt bog, a dump, of no value: the site preparation for 1939 was a major land reclamation effort. Today, the cry might very well be one for *restoring* the area as a tidal wetland. But first the groundwater would have to be checked for contaminants from Fishhook McCarthy's old dump.

The New Frontiers of Experience

Almost the first step taken by any city planning a world's fair is to ensure that the new exposition will have its own theme multi-media, IMAX production (for example, *Energy* for the 1982 Knoxville Fair). The 1964/65 World's Fair first established the drawing power of the indelible experiences such technologies can provide. A formidable battery of strikingly novel cinematic displays, exhibitry techniques, and multi-media special-effect rides awaited the fairgoer. This dazzling display of technical wizardry remains one of the Fair's most memorable legacies. The "experience technologies" have had a lasting and controversial influence.

Francis Thompson and Alexander Hamid's *To Be Alive,* in the Johnson Wax pavilion, stunningly used three eighteen-foot-wide screens to capture scenes of ordinary life from around the world, from childhood to old age. The screens gracefully interplayed: three identical images, for example, would turn into one extended image or three distinct images. Saul Bass's *From Here to There,* at United Airlines (in Transportation and Travel), projected scenes of parting and arrival in airports in sepia tones that were suddenly interspersed with full-color, wide-screen aerial views from a jet. His twenty-three-minute *The Searching Eye* at Eastman Kodak projected the views of a boy exploring the world around him in 35mm, and showed us what the boy sees and doesn't see in 70mm.

"Past as Prologue," the United States pavilion's extravaganza, viewed on moving grandstands, led one through American history and to the moon and Milky Way with 135 screens that rose, slid, and formed tunnels. As noted, GE's Skydome Spectacular focused 87 tandem projectors on its giant hemispherical dome, and Charles Eames's fourteen screens (canted at polyhedral angles) and nine projectors deluged audiences with rapidly cut sequences of simultaneous images of different aspects of a subject; separate screens, for example, showed a gyrating speedometer, a cheering crowd,

Below, top: Underwater cities were projected for the future, and included vacation resorts, oil drilling facilities and mineral mines. Inhabitants of such cities traveled by "aqua-scooter." Photograph courtesy of General Motors.

Below, bottom: Self-propelled mobile homes, for life in the "Futurama" jungle, featured expandable living compartments. Photograph courtesy of General Motors.

spinning tires, and a racer crouched over a wheel. Eames used this kaleidoscopic technique to illustrate the nature of abstraction and problem-solving, and to prove by its own example that people come away with different experiences of the same event. Cylindrical screens (with the audience inside) were used in the New York State pavilion's Theaterama film, which took one to Niagara Falls and other attractions.

These and other techniques, deployed with artistry, can qualitatively alter the character of one's aesthetic experience. There are *kinds* of experiences one can get only from a particular medium of expression—reading, storytelling, film, videotape, holography, music, etc.[20] The new forms of experience emerging from the Fair technologies, including those combining film with multi-media shows, laser shows, and sound effects, might be said to include heightened experiences of this sort: (a) visceral illusions, such as one gets sitting close to an IMAX or Omnimax screen: the palpable feeling of centrifugal force as one "drives" sharply winding roads at high speed, the vertiginous feeling as one "glides" over the crest of Niagara Falls; (b) the feeling of depth and dimensionality from cylindrical and spherical screens (exploited now by Omnimax); (c) the staccato feeling of fragmentation, confusion, and irritation from cuts so rapid one cannot "follow" things, or from information overload from too many screens bombarding one with too much "information" at once; (d) experiencing an event from several emotional or physical perspectives, as in the Saul Bass films; and (e) childlike sensual delight in the sheer display of pattern and color. Needless to say, used artlessly or to excess, the media technologies that were the hallmark of the Fair become empty, annoying clichés or passing curiosities.

There are some footnotes to the

Below: The interior of the Port Authority Heliport featured a twelve-minute film about transportation projected on a 195-foot, circular screen. Photograph by the Port Authority of New York. Courtesy of Peter M. Warner.

Fair's cinema legacy. The Billy Graham pavilion's twenty-eight-minute spectacular, *Man in the Fifth Dimension,* portrayed the wonders of space and atom in 70 millimeters on a somewhat curved screen; as with IBM's film, headsets were available at many seats for simultaneous translations into the language one dialed. Du Pont's musical was coordinated with a film in which, for example, a screen actor would appear to hand a rose to a live actor. Olfactory technology was "deployed" in Coca-Cola's scented Taj Mahal, Bavarian Ski Lodge, Hong Kong Street, Rio Harbor, and Cambodian Forest.

Computer- and analogue-device-driven technologies for synchronization and control of several projectors, moving screens, and speakers in three dimensions were the key ingredients in many of the Fair's cinematic experiments. The same control technologies were instrumental in the development of the Fair's touted Disney "Audio-Animatronic" exhibits. Since the Fair, this kind of technology has improved by leaps and bounds, especially in Hollywood, with the help of miniaturization and microprocessor technology.

Disney also designed the huge Ford Wonder Rotunda (the largest building at the Fair—GM had the biggest site) and Ford's "Magic Skyway," which visitors rode in one of 160 real convertibles polished between every trip. Fairs can be exhausting, so the chance to sit down must have added to the popularity of the rides.

After the Fair, the people-moving, "Audio-Animatronic," and cinematic technologies were used by Disney and other theme parks. EPCOT Center in particular is in many ways a Fair legacy. IMAX and other descendants of Fair technologies have become staples at science museums all over North America.

Yesterday's New Frontiers Today

While automobiles, television, and airplanes received a great deal of attention at the Fair, by 1964 they were fixtures of the technological landscape, with impacts spread throughout society—anything but *New* Frontiers. The true frontier technologies of the Fair, however, are still in their infancy; they might be called Old Frontiers. When it comes to computers and space travel, fission and fusion power, and a new generation of incredibly exotic materials, one hasn't seen everything yet—assuming, that is, that one chooses to continue pursuing these technologies. And two other revolutionary technologies have appeared since 1964: biotechnology and high-temperature superconductivity.

How can these technologies be guided wisely? One lesson to be drawn from the history of technology and society since 1964 is that Americans are only beginning to appreciate the moral dilemmas they present. As those which have been sketched here suggest, values are indispensible in making decisions about the course of technology. Science can't make the choice, if only because scientific disagreement on the capabilities and risks of each technology is not going to go away. There are no Mr. Spocks: one might say, rather, "two experts, three opinions." So people are thrown back again and again on their values: what's fair? what's a worthy goal? what technology seems best matched to people and communities?

Another lesson learned since 1964/65 is that while technologies exhibited at the Fair have improved life dramatically, they also pose environmental risks, in many cases on a planetary scale. The societal impacts of genetic and computer technology are likely to be equally portentous. Squarely addressing these concerns requires courage *and* circumspection.

Citizens can best weigh the competing scientific arguments and assay the value issues by becoming well-versed in science and technology *and* in philosophy and history. Citizens should be judges, not consumers of expertise. This is why the educational mission of world's fairs is so important.

The 1964/65 Fair's *Official Souvenir Book* declared, "Without pause, man has rushed headlong into the nuclear age, the space age, and the age of automation."[21] Society's attitude toward the impact of technology now seems to be in a generally cautionary phase, and so this statement is interpreted as a criticism. What's striking is that in 1964 the words were meant as praise: praise for not acting halfheartedly or dillydallying around. That is why looking back to the confident world of 1964 is instructive. It puts things into perspective by reminding one that these things—confidence, caution—come and go. And who does not yearn for confidence?

Below, top: A scene from the "Global Holiday" exhibit in the Coca-Cola pavilion. A bustling Hong Kong street was one of five recreations of "exotic" places around the world. The sights, sounds, climates, and aromas of Rio de Janeiro, a Bavarian ski lodge, a serene Indian garden, and a Cambodian forest were also featured. Photograph courtesy of Peter M. Warner.

Below, bottom: Amphicar, "the car that swims", was demonstrated at the Lake Amusement area of the Fair. Photograph courtesy of Peter M. Warner.

Cornell Capa, *Billy
Graham Pavilion.* The Fair
featured many religious
pavilions. Graham's was
designed by Edward
Durrell Stone. Photograph
courtesy of Cornell
Capa/Magnum Photos Inc.

The "Laissez-Fair," Good Taste, and Money Trees: Architecture at the Fair

Rosemarie Haag Bletter

Previews of the New York World's Fair of 1964 in the professional architecture and design journals were for the most part not kind. *Architectural Forum* announced "The Arrested Development of the New York Fair," *Industrial Design* editorialized "The Fair is (So Far) Foul," and *Craft Horizons* was the most succinct, with "The Laissez-Fair."[1] Reviews of the Fair, once it opened, were not much kinder; the criticism only became more specific. The 1964/65 Fair never achieved the iconic impact of the 1939/40 Fair, which in retrospect has attained a rosy glow as the great public entertainment celebrating the end of the Depression. Its professional reception was in fact negative at the time as well. One critic referred to its architecture as "Corporation Style."[2] In reality it was the onset of World War II, four months after the Fair opened, that ended the Depression, but that hardly matters today. The Fair of 1939 fulfills one of those conveniently uplifting caesuras between two cataclysmic events, insuring it the limelight of memory. The Fair of 1964/65 cannot be bracketed so neatly. Some of its aspects still reflected the Cold War of the Eisenhower and Kennedy years, and its conception took place too early to partake fully in the counterculture that developed in the later sixties.

The 1964/65 World's Fair and its image were controlled by Robert Moses and his dedication to turning a profit. The Fair Corporation had appointed a design committee consisting of architects Wallace K. Harrison, Gordon Bunshaft, Edward Durrell Stone, designer Henry Dreyfuss, and engineer Emil Praeger. The design committee had proposed a single, doughnut-shaped building in which the various exhibits would be housed. Moses was appointed President of the Fair Corporation in 1960 at a hefty salary of $100,000 (Mayor Robert F. Wagner, Jr., was earning only $40,000 then). In order to assume his new job, Moses was required to resign from his New York City jobs, an action welcomed by the mayor's office since Moses had come under increasing criticism during the late fifties.[3]

Moses spurned the design committee's proposal as impractical and too much like the centralized pavilion at the Universal Exposition of 1867 in Paris.[4] The reason for his rejection of this design, however, was more likely financial: the Fair Corporation did not want to be responsible for such a large building. It was widely believed that the reason the 1939/40 Fair had lost money was because the Fair Corporation had erected too many buildings with its own funds. To further complicate the matter,

the Paris-based Bureau of International Expositions requires that the first five thousand square feet of exhibit space for each country must be rent-free and that an officially sanctioned world's fair must take place within a single year and not be extended into a second. Because the Fair Corporation was adamant in not giving in on these points, the 1964/65 Fair was not approved by this international body—a condition that had been so in 1939/40 as well, though then Fair President Grover Whalen had done his best to persuade foreign countries to participate despite the lack of an official sanction.[5]

The Fair Corporation spent lavishly. Thomas Deegan, a public relations man and an ally of Moses, stated publicly that, "I . . . expect to continue to serve [the 1964 Fair Corporation] without any fees or expenses of any kind." Nonetheless, he received a $100,000 salary, expenses for a $1,000-a-month suite in the Waldorf, and $572 for a chauffeur, and his public relations firm was awarded a further fee of $350,000 per year. Moses also spent the astronomical sum of nearly $10,000,000 for security during the 1964/65 Fair's first year. The normal hourly wage set for the Fair's carpenters was $23, with $17 an hour for garbage collectors.[6] Because rental charges and other services were exorbitant, not many foreign countries were willing to participate.

The themes of the 1964/65 Fair were "Peace through understanding" and "Man's achievements on a shrinking globe in an expanding universe." As one commentator pointed out in 1961:

At last reports, the globe was shrinking more rapidly than Robert Moses . . . realized: Italy, France [and] Great Britain . . . had announced they would not participate . . . and there were signs that most of Western Europe would refuse to join in the little world of Robert Moses.[7]

After the design committee submitted a second, pared-down version for a single structure, which was rejected by the Fair Corporation as well, it resigned. In its

place, the Fair Corporation created a "Committee on Conformity," whose chairman (on the recommendation of Moses) was Major General Thomas F. Farrell, an engineering consultant, a former chairman of the New York City Housing Authority, and a former deputy commander of the Manhattan Project for developing the atomic bomb.[8] In the wake of the design committee's resignation, the critic Douglas Haskell complained in *Architectural Forum* that "the fair layout has been done virtually by lawyers who have told lessors what could be built and where, by interpreting mechanical rules concerning building lines and free space between structures."[9] The Fair's general plan simply reused the ground plan of its 1939/40 predecessor.

Because the 1964 Fair Corporation chose not to impose a unifying approach, the resulting messy melange of buildings actually demonstrated Moses's accommodation to free-market competition. A display of commercial might is, of course, never totally absent from any international exhibition. This kind of competition was perhaps not as clearly expressed architecturally in the fairs of the second half of the nineteenth century, when various competing displays were (at least from the exterior) brought together under one great structure. In the twentieth century, national pavilions multiplied, and beginning with the New York World's Fair of 1939/40, national pavilions were overwhelmed by corporate buildings. The same was true in 1964, because neither fair had a full complement of foreign nations.

Despite its inauspicious beginning, the 1964/65 Fair, especially in its more futuristic designs, tells us a great deal about the expectations and beliefs that were current in the years of its inception. When the Fair opened, *Holiday* magazine advised its readers, with tongue in cheek, that "It is precisely the chaos of architectural styles that lends to Flushing

Below: Spain's pavilion designed by Javier Carvajal Ferrer and Kelly & Gruzen. Photography by J. Alex Langley, courtesy of Gruzen, Samton, Steinglass, architects.

Below, bottom: Courtyard of the Spain pavilion. Photography courtesy of Gruzen, Samton, Steinglass, architects.

Meadow the nightmare quality any proper World's Fair should strive for."[10]

Industrial Design reported that the Fair had a "lack of a sense of scale and a range of design that runs the gamut from the visionary to the ridiculous."[11] Harsher estimates were more characteristic in architectural journals, such as Douglas Haskell's editorial in *Architectural Forum:*

Where there has been no point or purpose except to make money the outcome has been like that of the recent fair in Brussels. In its failure to establish anything but chaos out of the scheme as a whole, despite brilliant individual efforts, this fair made the country that organized it look disorganized. [The Brussels Fair took place in 1958.]

Fairs are slightly more important than children's amusement parks or adults' swimming beaches in what they seek to do, and unexpected revelations come out of the way they do it. In a world looking for new ways of organizing big environments, even big play spaces, the New York World's Fair threatens to convey an impression of immaturity and arrested cultural development that many foreign observers will ascribe to the U.S. as a whole.[12]

Though the 1964 Fair is not remembered with the same fondness as that of 1939, several of its individual pavilions were designed by noteworthy architects. The quiet dignity of the Spanish pavilion made it stand out against the surrounding clutter. Designed by Javier Carvajal Ferrer with the New York architectural firm of Kelly & Gruzen, it was the Fair's most widely praised structure.[13] Its precast concrete facade was rather bland and institutional, but like traditional Spanish houses, it turned its back to the street. Its luxurious displays were contained in two sun-filled patios and in elegant, dark, and dramatically lit rooms. The ceiling was covered with 350,000 small wooden blocks that were placed at varying heights, creating a richly textured, Moorish-inspired honeycomb effect. The coherent design and the emphasis on high culture were reinforced by an exhibition of paintings by such artists as Velázquez, Goya, and Miró, photographs of contemporary Spanish architecture, projects by young architecture students, and even Balenciaga-designed hostess uniforms.

Below: Japan pavilion designed by Kunio Mayekawa. The stone walls were created by sculptor Masayuki Nagare. Photographs courtesy of Oppenheimer, Brady & Vogelstein.

Opposite: The Japan pavilion contained displays of advanced technologies. Shown is a demonstration of an NEC scrambler phone. Photograph courtesy of the Rare Books and Manuscripts Division, New York Public Library, Astor, Lenox, and Tilden Foundations.

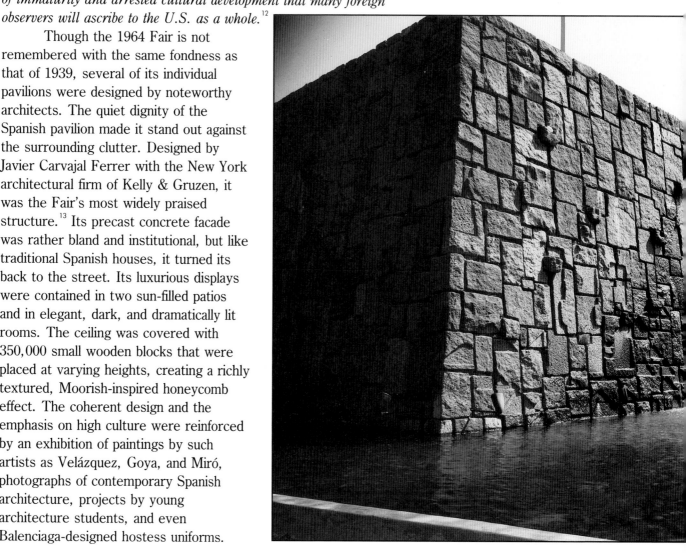

The Japanese pavilion by architect Kunio Mayekawa, like Carvajal's design, had a somewhat forbidding exterior. The stone walls by sculptor Masayuki Nagare seemed to reinterpret the fortified castles of the Shoguns more than they conveyed the lightness of Japanese imperial architecture. The tradition-inspired facade contrasted with an aggressive display of high technology that troubled many architecture critics. *Progressive Architecture* informed its readers that "A good-looking main pavilion by Kunio Mayekawa with handsome sculptured stone walls by Nagare is let down by overindustrialized exhibits."[14] In retrospect, this emphasis on industrialization prefigured Japan's later role in the world economy.

Both the Spanish and Japanese pavilions were singled out by critics as tasteful, well-designed buildings, but they probably did not make as strong an impression on the general public. Much more in the spirit of a lively amusement fair was the IBM pavilion, designed by Eero Saarinen & Associates in collaboration with the designer Charles Eames (Saarinen died in 1961 and the structure was completed by his successors, Kevin Roche and John Dinkeloo). A large white ellipsoid, which contained a multi-screen projection theater, seemed to rest like an egg in a nest, on a grove of stylized steel trees. The exterior of the ovoid auditorium was covered completely with a relief pattern of the letters IBM, suggesting the notion of information in general and, more specifically, the company's new Selectric typewriter, in which a lettered ball replaced the older type keys. (The Selectric could be tested by the public at the "Typewriter Bar.")

This pavilion was conceived by its designers as a "non-architectural" assemblage of spaces and as an "environment." At many of its points and in the way traffic flow was handled, the

indirect message was that apparent chaos can lead to order. This was demonstrated most expertly in the jumbled "maze," where visitors queued up in seeming disorder, but then filed into the neat rows of seats of the "people wall," a hydraulic, computer-engineered bleacher seating system that lifted the audience up into the "information center," the ellipsoid auditorium. There was also a "probability machine," like a giant pinball game in which thousands of plastic balls were dropped from the top into compartments below. The regular and predictable distribution of balls was meant to demonstrate how science makes use of chance to detect the laws of order.[15]

High technology was present, but played down, in the IBM pavilion's base, which was described as a "garden grove" of tree-like, weathering-steel structures, covered by a gray-green translucent plastic. Cor-Ten Steel, the outer layers of which have intentionally been allowed to rust forming a protective layer, makes steel look mellow and textured rather than sleek and mechanistic. Together with the arbored forms inspired by nature, the non-architectural approach to design, and the open structure at the base that allowed visitors to move freely between the display kiosks—many interactive, such as the "Typewriter Bar," where the public was encouraged to write postcards to friends—all seemed to forecast the spirit of the later sixties in the designers' attempt to humanize technology.

Throughout the displays at the IBM pavilion, an effort was made for computers and other technology to seem less unfriendly and mysterious. One kiosk featured a computer that translated from Russian to "understandable English." Before the "people wall" ascended in full view of Fair visitors into the "information machine," a "host" was lowered on a tiny circular platform to greet the visitors; he then reappeared inside the auditorium to personalize the rapid-fire multi-screen

Below, top and opposite top: IBM pavilion designed by Eero Saarinen, completed by Kevin Roche & John Dinkeloo. The main feature of the pavilion was the ninety-foot-high, egg-shaped theater. Photograph courtesy of Kevin Roche, John Dinkeloo and Associates.

Below, bottom: Detail of the architectural support of the IBM pavilion. Forty-five rust-colored "trees" formed the base of the pavilion. Photograph courtesy of Kevin Roche, John Dinkeloo and Associates.

Opposite bottom: Detail of the People Wall, IBM pavilion. Upon entrance to the pavilion, up to 500 visitors sat on enormous bleachers, which hyraulically moved up into the theater. Photograph by Gert Berliner.

images. The presentation opened with ordinary information about the master of ceremonies: what he had for breakfast, a view of his closet at home and his credit card, and a chat with his mother.[16] Architectural historian Vincent Scully described the host on his suspended platform with his inimitable mythomania:

[As the visitors ascended they were] cheered on by a splendid fellow who began the whole business by appearing before you high on a platform let down from the egg—like a jolly young god, triumphant over gravity. . . . In this punctual **deus ex machina** *the designers have hit a Dionysian button, calling up emotions of awe, terror, recognition and joy that are far more religious than those which Michelangelo's* **Pietà** *evokes in its present shameful setting.*[17]

Much of the credit for the amusement-park-style entertainment of the IBM pavilion must go to Charles Eames, who, after his early work as an architect and furniture designer, had increasingly become interested in transmitting scientifically complex theories to a general public, especially in a series of acclaimed educational films.

When Saarinen received the commission for the IBM pavilion, he was at the height of his fame, having completed such Neo-Expressionist structures as the TWA Terminal at Kennedy Airport (1956–62), Dulles International Airport, Chantilly, Virginia (1958–62), as well as several corporate headquarters, among them the subtle John Deere & Co. Headquarters, Moline, Illinois (1957–63) and the much more conservative Thomas J. Watson Research Center for IBM, Yorktown, New York (1957–61). Roche & Dinkeloo, which became the successor firm to Saarinen & Associates, went on to design the stunning Ford Foundation Headquarters, New York (1963–68), which introduced the first large glass-enclosed garden court within an urban structure. The IBM pavilion remains an important work in Saarinen's career as well as that of Roche & Dinkeloo. As *Progressive Architecture* reported in 1964, it was "one of the few [at the Fair] that didn't lay an egg."[18]

Like the IBM pavilion, the New York State pavilion, designed by Philip Johnson and Richard Foster, merited praise from the architectural profession, particularly for its cable-hung roof, which was the largest in the world. It was also lauded for its "grand, gaudy circus-tent" atmosphere."[19] The oval suspended roof was assembled on the ground and then jacked up into place; like the IBM pavilion's steel trees, it was covered with translucent plastic, but here in the bright colors of a stained-glass window. The disc-topped towers of the New York State pavilion (the highest structure at the Fair) made the design appear to be an informal assemblage of parts, yet it contained none of the open-ended, interactive features of the IBM pavilion. Instead, the huge scale of the reinforced concrete columns supporting the roof prefigured the crushing, Egyptian-style monumentality of Johnson's later work.

Johnson's New York State pavilion seemed to be a reinterpretation of one of three proposals Frank Lloyd Wright produced as a defiant gesture when he was not invited to participate in the 1933 Chicago Century of Progress Exposition:

Opposite: Detail of the two towers of the New York State pavilion. The tallest structures at the Fair, these towers housed an observation platform and a restaurant. Photograph by Anthony P. Manfre.

Below: New York State pavilion designed by Philip Johnson. Photograph by Bob Golby, collection of The Queens Museum.

A weaving characteristic of this age of steel in tension. Accept from John Roebling his pioneer work—message of the Brooklyn Bridge. Build noble pylons . . . on the Lake Front five hundred feet apart . . . This plastic-slung canopy to be anchored by steel cables to the outer series of appropriate pylons. Weave, in the main and minor and intermediate cables, a network that would support transparent fabrications such as we have as modern glass substitutes in our day. Thus make an architectural canopy more beautiful and more vast than any ever seen.[20]

The most futuristic design of both the 1939/40 and 1964/65 fairs was not an individual building, but General Motors's "Futurama" exhibit. In both instances it fulfilled most completely the expectations of the "visionary," predictive element of an international exhibition. Each "Futurama" exhibit was the most popular display of its respective fair. The exhibits consisted of large, elaborate models showing a future "real" world that visitors circumnavigated in moving "sound" chairs, looking down on the model as if from some aerial perspective while being informed by recordings as to what they were seeing. In 1939 the "Futurama" model was housed inside a building by the architect Albert Kahn. The exhibit itself was designed by the noted industrial designer Norman Bel Geddes. It showed ribbons of superhighways crisscrossing the continental United States, and, according to the taped message, benefiting farmers and industrial communities. This "skyride" ended with a view of a metropolis with streamlined skyscrapers interspersed between low-rise buildings, parks, and more highways. The recorded voice told the visitor about "the city of 1960, with its abundant sunshine, fresh air, fine green parkways—all the result of thoughtful planning and design."[21]

In terms of planning, Bel Geddes's design for 1939 combined the urbanistic projects of Le Corbusier of the twenties and thirties with Frank Lloyd Wright's scheme for Broadacre City, begun in the mid-thirties, which was more rural than Le Corbusier's (yet both Le Corbusier

Below, top and bottom:
The 1939/40 "Futurama"
projected a future where
seven-lane highways,
designed to accomodate
traffic at 100 miles per
hour, were commonplace.
Photographs courtesy of
General Motors.

and Wright had relied on the superhighway as their communities' connective spines). In 1939, the "Futurama" had predicted 38 million cars for America in 1960. By 1960 there were in fact 61 million cars, almost twice as many as projected,[22] and without any of the accompanying "thoughtful planning" promised in 1939.

In 1964 the General Motors Building was again designed by Albert Kahn Associates (Kahn himself had died in 1942). The structure was fronted by a huge, ten-story forward-cantilevered and curving wall of aluminum-clad spars. Since it was inclined away from the building's footprint, it is vaguely reminiscent of Eric Mendelsohn's gravity-defying projects of the 1910s. *Progressive Architecture* noted another, more literal connection to its period by dubbing the building "Miss Tailfin of 1964–5."[23]

Like the earlier "Futurama," the 1964/65 version was, of course, a dramatic advertisement for facilitating the spread of the automobile. The general corporate atmosphere of the 1964/65 Fair also pervaded General Motors's conception of the future. "Futurama" was designed by the General Motors styling staff; the scenes were constructed in a studio near Detroit, sawed into sections, trucked by a fleet of fifty trailers to New York, and reassembled like a gigantic jigsaw puzzle. Scenic backdrops were painted by artists from Metro-Goldwyn-Mayer. Thus, make-believe played an even larger role in 1964 than it had in 1939. The music that accompanied the voice of the sound chairs was appropriately written by a jingle writer, James Fagas, described in a General Motors press release as:

. . . one of a small, uniquely-talented group of composers able to augment visual or audible images with musical sounds to help create a favorable impression for the product whose praises . . . are being sung.

"The music can't be too good," Fagas explained. "It must highlight the product,

Below: The 1964 version of the "Futurama" also featured sound-equipped chairs. Visitors moved through six environments: "A trip to the moon," "Life under ice," "Underwater scene," "Visiting the jungle," "In the desert," and "The city of the future." These views (top and bottom left) depict scenes from "Life under ice." Workmen in Antartica install an under-ice laboratory. Photographs courtesy of General Motors.

Below, bottom right: The "Visiting the jungle" environment featured a freight depot with containerized shipments of lumber, chemicals and other materials. Photograph courtesy of General Motors.

Opposite, top: The undersea environment of the General Motors "Futurama" depicted an underwater hotel and a "sportsman" traveling by "aqua-scooter." Photograph courtesy of General Motors.

Opposite, bottom: "In the desert" showed electronic and computerized farming of reclaimed desert wasteland irrigated with desalted sea water. Photograph courtesy of General Motors.

but it must not steal its identity."

For the exterior landscaping of the General Motors Building, an organic material was used as mulch: seven hundred cubic yards of coffee grounds from a local instant coffee factory—"enough," the General Motors press release went on, "to make 32 million cups of coffee." Terrain for the "Futurama" model, on the other hand, was made of powdered asbestos. The hazardous artificiality of the model itself extended to the whole conception of a future world. Ostensibly concerned with an ever-growing population and a shrinking globe, superhighways, the car, and other technology were shown to have conquered the entire world, including the most inhospitable zones. Antarctica, "bleak, stark, uninhabited" and "twice the size of Australia" was one of the areas to be opened up to settlers by an all-weather harbor, a huge hole cut through the ice shelf, partly covered by a translucent, plastic hood to keep the water from freezing. "Atomic-powered submarine trains sail beneath the ice shelf and surface within the protected port." The plastic dome for climate control was comparable to one proposed by R. Buckminster Fuller as a "Partial Enclosure of Manhattan Island," which was exhibited in the Museum of Modern Art's "Visionary Architecture" show of 1960.[24]

More in line with the global extension of the car was the "Futurama's" presentation of the world's jungles. The General Motors designers proposed replacing the jungles' main artery—the "aimlessly wandering river"—with big highways. The motorway was to be cleared by a tree-clipper with laser beams.[25] Spraying the cleared areas with chemicals would be followed by a "road-builder," five stories high and three football fields long, "capable of producing from within itself one mile of four-lane, elevated superhighway every hour." In

Left and below: "The city of the future" had easy and quick mid-town parking, super skyscrapers, and intercontinental highways. Photographs courtesy of General Motors.

effect, the "road-builder" was a mobile factory applying mass-production techniques to the construction of highways. "General Motors' designers feel mobile atomic reactors or a number of other electric-generating devices . . . would be more than adequate." There were also proposals for remote-control farms in the desert, with water pumped in by atomic-generated electricity, as well as for the underwater construction of hotels and other large buildings.

Most astonishingly, General Motors declared: "The city, which long strove for growth, is imperiled by its own excesses. The suburbs are emerging as the centers of communal living." The flight to the suburbs was true enough, but it had been made possible precisely because of the propaganda for the private car and the expansion of the highway system popularized by the 1939 "Futurama." That cities became "imperiled by their own excesses" is a curious displacement of events. To get more cars onto existing motorways, the 1964 "Futurama" included an "autoline" of automatically controlled cars that would "substantially increase highway capacity by reducing the space between vehicles"; furthermore, "family vehicles, equipped with television, stereo, game table and refrigerator for passenger enjoyment, speed to their destination without manual control when operating in the 'autoline' lane." To cope with and satisfy women's special function as "poor drivers" and "avid shoppers," General Motors exhibited throughout shopping areas the "easily maneuverable, three-wheeled 'Runabouts,' especially designed for housewives," which included "a built-in, removable, shopping cart.

Of all the "visionary" proposals included in the 1964/65 "Futurama," it was containerization, the efficient shipment of goods via standard-size containers that fit railroad flatbeds or trucks, that has been realized most fully,

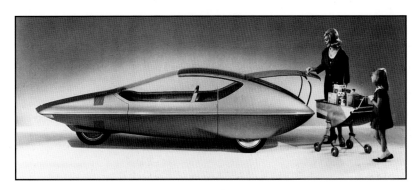

though not in the organized fashion predicted. "Futurama" showed open, high-rise warehouses for the orderly storage of containers, but today, as containers are transferred from ships and before they are attached to trucks or railroad cars, they are commonly stacked in huge parking lots—a cheaper way to deal with the process. (The present-day need for large open spaces to hold containers has had a detrimental impact on old port cities such as New York, which have lost out to newer port areas such as New Jersey.) In this respect, containerization has had the same kind of negative effect on the man-made environment as the car. Just as we are capable of building garages to contain the spread of the parking lot, they are often not built because it is cheaper to cover a site with tarmac than it is to erect a multi-story structure.

It is noteworthy that the "Futurama" exhibit did not take containerization into a more truly visionary realm. General Motors's prosaic proposals for container warehouses might, for example, be contrasted with projects by a number of Italian architects displayed at the Museum of Modern Art's "Italy: The New Domestic Landscape" exhibition in 1972. There Marco Zanuso and Richard Sapper showed a modified container unit that could serve as temporary housing, an imaginative alternative to the house trailer which comes with wheels that are almost never needed after the initial shipping to its site. Conventional mobile homes are bought because they constitute inexpensive housing, not because their occupants want to travel around the country (only vacation trailers need their built-in mobility).[26] The container, outfitted as a living unit, could conceivably provide more economical temporary quarters than the house trailer because it can be piggybacked to its site by train or truck.

One 1964 pavilion that seemed, on the surface, to fit the futuristic tradition of world's fairs was the Port Authority heliport erected by the Port of New York Authority. It had a restaurant and helicopter landing pad raised high above the ground by symmetrically placed supports that also contained elevators and other services. As an architectural design, however, the Port Authority structure is static and not nearly as revolutionary in its conception as El Lissitzky's dynamic proposals of 1924 for "Cloudhangers," asymmetrically cantilevered buildings that were to straddle existing Moscow streets. The inclusion of landing pads within the city or on building roofs has an even longer tradition that began with Antonio Sant'Elia's futurist designs for his *Citta Nuova* of 1912–14 and extended through Le Corbusier's urban schemes of the twenties, down to Frank Lloyd Wright's late designs for Broadacre City made in the fifties. An actual helicopter landing pad had been included atop the recently completed Pan Am Building, New York (1963) by Emery Roth & Sons, Pietro Belluschi, and Walter Gropius. Helicopter landings there were later abandoned, however, after a fatal accident proved them too dangerous for midtown Manhattan. *Progressive Architecture* correctly assessed the status of the Port Authority heliport when it commented: "Another building that will remain after the fair, sad to say."[27]

More adventurous than the Port Authority heliport, but never carried out, was the scheme for the "Galaxon" Space Park and Moon-Viewing Platform, commissioned by the Portland Cement Association and designed by Paul Rudolph, then dean of the School of Architecture at Yale. It had been a competing design for the Fair's theme center. The project was for an inclined viewing platform consisting of prestressed, precast concrete elements cantilevered from a central ring and column. Structurally more exhibitionist

Port Authority Heliport, designed by the Port of New York Authority. This building remains in Flushing Meadow Park and serves as a catering facility. Photograph by Bob Golby, collection of The Queens Museum.

than the IBM pavilion's hydraulic "people wall," it would have looked like a giant telescope in which visitors could enter the "saucer" to observe heavenly events. According to Rudolph, the "Galaxon" was also to include powerful light beacons directed toward outer space.[28]

The generically named "Pavilion" by the architectural firm of Eggers & Higgins and designed by Synergetics, Inc., a firm with which R. Buckminster Fuller had at one time been associated, seemed to be an abbreviated version of Fuller's geodesic domes. Fuller had erected geodesic domes since the late forties, but his design for the United States pavilion at Montreal in 1967 represented the largest and most visible example of such a structure. The Pavilion, used for general assemblies in 1964, became the Winston Churchill Pavilion after the statesman's death in 1965 because Robert Moses wanted to increase attendance with a Churchill memorial exhibition after it became clear that the Fair was not the financial success he had predicted.

Other structurally advanced buildings at the 1964/65 Fair were the General Electric pavilion by Welton Becket Associates, which had an unusual lamella dome with a suspended roof,[29] and the West Berlin pavilion by Ludwig Thürmer, which employed plastic tenting in the manner of Frei Otto,[30] a system that was made better known in Otto's design for the German pavilion at Expo '67 in Montreal.

A large number of buildings also looked back to the past, some with a characteristic 1950s futuristic look. Most typical of these was Johnson Wax by Lippincott & Margulies. It had the flying-saucer style of some of Wright's late works, such as his project for a Huntington Hartford Play Resort of 1947. Welton Becket Associates' Coca-Cola Building, on the other hand, with its needle-like projections, looked more like

Opposite, top: General Electric pavilion designed by Welton Becket Associates. Photograph courtesy of General Electric.
Opposite, bottom: Johnson Wax pavilion designed by Lippincott & Margulies Photograph courtesy of Peter M. Warner.

Right: Mormon Church designed by Fordyce & Hamby Associates. Photograph courtesy of Photofest.
Below: The "Pavilion," renamed the Churchill Center during the 1965 season of the Fair, housed a memorial to Winston Churchill. Photograph by Peter M. Warner.

the spiky futurism of early buildings at Disneyland.

Encouraged by Moses, the abundance of religious pavilions at the 1964/65 Fair—he had wanted a more wholesome image than that created by the honky-tonk of the entertainment zone of 1939—did not make for fun-house architecture. With the Billy Graham pavilion by Edward Durell Stone, the Christian Science pavilion by the same architect, the Mormon Church pavilion by Fordyce & Hamby (basically a large facade of the Mormon Tabernacle in Salt Lake City), and several others, any atmosphere of hearty entertainment was in effect stifled. Even more strait-laced than the religious pavilions was the Hall of Free Enterprise, an abstracted classical temple by the architect Ira Kessler that fully prefigured the cardboardy thinness of later American Post-Modern Classicism. In many ways the Fair revealed a strange conjunction of corporate America and Christian sectarianism that we might more readily associate with the Reagan years of the eighties.

The "Progressland" show inside the General Electric pavilion ended with an "actual demonstration of thermonuclear fusion" that took place every fifteen minutes. It was the first time nuclear fusion was demonstrated for a public audience.[31] Though "the wonders of atomic energy" were alluded to in several of the Fair exhibits, a darker response to the fear of atomic energy also manifested itself in the design of the Underground World Home designed by the architects Billy J. Cox and Don L. Kittrell. *Progressive Architecture* noted that the Underground World Home was meant as protection against radiation fallout and more benign pollution such as pollen.[32] The Underground Home had been the idea of a Texas builder, Jay Swayze, president of the Underground World Home Corporation. He had been a contractor of luxury houses when the

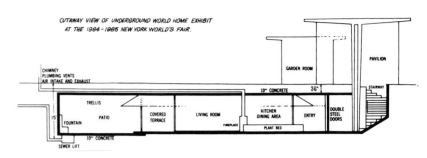

CUTAWAY VIEW OF UNDERGROUND WORLD HOME EXHIBIT AT THE 1964-1965 NEW YORK WORLD'S FAIR.

Opposite: Cut-away view of the Underground World Home pavilion. Photograph courtesy of Peter M. Warner.

Below: Patio of the Underground World Home. The advantages of living underground were promoted in this pavilion. Control over climate and noise, and protection from fire and radiation were the key features. Photograph courtesy of Photofest.

Below, top right: Entrance to the Underground World Home. Photograph courtesy of Peter M. Warner.

Below, center and bottom: View of the bedrooms, Underground World Home. The interiors of the pavilion were designed by Marilynn Motto. Photographs courtesy of Peter M. Warner.

Cuban Missile Crisis occurred in 1962. The Plainview, Texas, City Council commissioned a fallout shelter from him to specifications by the Department of Civil Defense. He wrote about this in 1980:

I saw the merit of utilizing the earth as protection against radioactive fallout. As a former military instructor in chemical warfare, I knew that the three ways man could destroy himself were by nuclear fission, nerve gas, or germ warfare. Despite President Kennedy's assurance that the threat of war was only temporary, one thing was clear. The nuclear age was upon us, and long-range planning was necessary to protect humanity from possible ill effects.[33]

Swayze then developed a survey to find out how much value was placed on windows, and he found that the "average family prepares for work or school in the morning without glancing outside . . . and in the evening simply reverses this process." He observed that actual views were often uninspiring (showing other buildings or "dusty skies"). Further, he noted, "we sleep one third of our lives with our eyes closed, seeing nothing at all." He concluded that psychologically, windows may be needed, but are in fact rarely looked at. "I decided an artist could do a thousand times better."[34]

Swayze did his first full-fledged underground house in 1962; it was much larger than the bomb shelter he had done for Plainview. The house was two to three feet underground, and only its double garage was above grade. The main entry to the house below was between the two garage doors. The concept of the house with only the garage visible represented an extreme progression of the garage being attached to the service wing of the house as developed in the early twentieth century. Frank Lloyd Wright's Robie House, Chicago (1909) is a good instance of the garage as a vestige of the smelly stable. By the thirties, however, the garage had migrated to the front of the house, displacing the old front porch. At the same time, the front parlor became a back parlor, a more informal living room facing the private realm of the garden, as streets had become more noisy and unpleasant with the increasing presence of the car.[35] The Underground House took this development a step further: the garage is the only sign of human habitation that remained.

At the 1964 Fair, a somewhat smaller, traditional ranch-style version of Swayze's Underground House was put on display. It promised "Greater security—peace of mind—the ultimate in true privacy!"[36] It was "landscaped" on all four sides with terraces, backlit fences, and murals of natural settings that were described as "hideous" by one critic. One of the books on the Underground World Home bookshelf was *The U.S. Air Force Report on the Ballistic Missile.*[37] By the time Swayze wrote a book about his Underground House, *Underground Gardens and Homes: The Best of Two Worlds—Above and Below,* in 1980, the Cold War was over and his justification for going underground had become more ecological: underground houses preserve resources in a quickly expanding population. (He cited an 80-percent saving on heating and cooling costs.) In 1980 Swayze also proposed underground modular houses. He concluded that, although most people love nature, they do not want to take care of it. In the Underground World Home, the lawn never needed to be mowed. Light in the simulated out-of-doors was completely controlled from rheostats in each room: ". . . enabling each occupant . . . to change the exterior light . . . Choices are: sunlight, light simulating a rainy day, moonlight, or no light at all."[38]

The Fair's model houses were as much controlled by commercial considerations as was everything else in its domain. The "House of Good Taste," so named by Thomas Deegan, Robert Moses's public relations man, was really three houses: a "modern" house, designed by Edward Durell Stone; a "traditional" house by Royal Barry Wills;

and a "contemporary" house by Jack Pickens Coble. The traditional house had been the brainchild of Lady Malcolm Douglas-Hamilton, a well-connected socialite. She mentioned her idea for a house at the upcoming world's fair when she was seated next to Deegan at a dinner in Greenwich, Connecticut. The house should contain traditional furniture that could be bought anywhere in the country, she specified, and "a dining room—even a small one—as how can one teach children good table manners sitting at a kitchen counter? . . . There should be a Bible on the table beside the bed."[39] Deegan invited Lady Hamilton to be in charge of such a design and gave her a two-acre tract at the Fair.

Lady Hamilton's formal education had ended with finishing school, but once given the responsibility for overseeing this model house, she put together the "American Institute of Approval," a group of socially prominent advisers described as "nonprofessional women deeply interested in good taste."[40] When a few of her financial backers and some decorators exerted pressure to include more than just a traditional house, Lady Hamilton disagreed at first, claiming:

My whole concept had been a demonstration of middle-income, middle-of-the-road, traditional American good taste. Imitation modern can be pretentious, cheap looking, and in bad taste. The "best" modern, or even just good "modern," is extremely expensive and only for the very rich.[41]

In the end, Lady Hamilton relented, and approached the "dean of modern architecture," Edward Durell Stone. Stone had been the architect of the conservative United States pavilion at the Brussels World's Fair, and in 1965 he was to complete Huntington Hartford's Gallery of Modern Art, New York (now the New York City Department of Cultural Affairs). True to form, Stone adapted his modern house to the idea of a Pompeian villa: it was screened on the outside and looked inward toward a central pool covered by a translucent

Below, top: Floor plan and rendering of the Contemporary House designed by Jack Pickens Coble, House of Good Taste pavilion. Highlights of this house were: sliding glass doors, skylights, and a Finnish sauna. Photographs courtesy of Peter M. Warner.

Below, bottom: Floor plan and rendering of the Modern House designed by Edward Durrell Stone, House of Good Taste pavilion. This house included a patio at each corner, and a central family room and garden. Photographs courtesy of Peter M. Warner.

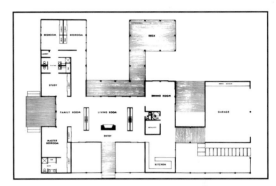

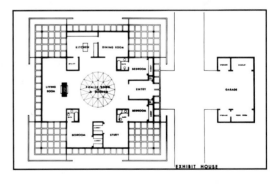

Below, top: Floor plan and rendering of the Traditional House designed by Royal Barry Wills for the House of Good Taste pavilion. Photographs courtesy of Peter M. Warner.

Below, bottom: Living Room, Traditional House. This house also had a party room with indoor barbecue/fireplace and a kitchen with a sewing nook.

dome. The soaring population problem was cited as the reason for this arrangement (one must remember that the 1964 time capsule included some of the newly developed birth control pills).[42] The Stone plan had complete four-part symmetry, giving it a veneer of Neoclassicism.

The "Contemporary House," using a more informal plan than the "Modern House," nevertheless also turned away from the street. Each one of the three houses was to cost between $30,000 and $40,000. Their interiors were done by professional decorators, but their furnishings had to be chosen from commercial exhibitors with national distribution.[43] *Interior Design* questioned the good taste of the "Modern" and "Traditional House," complaining about the "overemphasis on the display of merchandise," but praised the "Contemporary House" for its informality.[44] The juxtaposition of terms like "modern," "contemporary," and "traditional," especially where the "modern" house seemed quite traditional, is rather confusing, and it was no clearer for the visitor in 1964. *Holiday* magazine's reporter tried to get a clarification on this point from a guide; her answer was: "Contemporary is today," and "modern is tomorrow."[45] In other words, the future in 1964 was Pompeian. It should be added that in 1939 the Fair's model houses were not revolutionary either. "Tomorrow Town" at the 1939 Fair was meant to look like a New England village, with residential styles ranging from Colonial to Regency to modified Modern.[46]

The Formica Corporation exhibited its own contemporary house, which in its souvenir book was described as "advanced but not futuristic." The "Formica World's Fair House" was a ranch-style design by the architect Emil A. Schmidlin. It was one of six Formica prototypes intended to be erected in eighty-one locations throughout the

Left: The Town of Tomorrow, a community of demonstration houses at the 1939/40 Fair. Photograph courtesy of the New York Daily News.

Below: Backyard and pool, Traditional House, House of Good Taste pavilion. Photograph courtesy of Peter M. Warner.

United States in styles that repeated almost exactly the eclecticism of the 1939 Fair's "Town of Tomorrow": Cape Cod, Regency, traditional, ranch, etc.[47]

Formica, the laminated plastic, was referred to as "that wipe-clean wonder," and because the house's interiors were surfaced with the tough laminate, "juvenile wars may be fought amid this furniture."[48] The boy's room of the Formica House had a desk, "a great place to call his 'turf' but also an incentive to homework . . . a room that's youthful and male in every detail." In the girl's room, with pink wall paneling, there were "compact ready-made units under windows [that] convert to supports for sewing machine, typewriter, small ironing board." Nothing is said about incentives to do homework in the room. The four-poster bed in the girl's room also had a trundle bed, because "girls are gayer in twos."[49] The souvenir book described the kitchen as if the writer were some imaginary husband: "a kitchen that's in love with my wife . . ." The kitchen also contained a niche with a small built-in desk. As Formica described it:

The compact office, tucked into an out-of-the-way corner of the kitchen, takes no more space than a pantry closet but controls the entire house. Here menus are planned, groceries ordered, bills and files kept orderly. With housewide Miami-Carey intercom system, it's possible to answer the front door or speak to members of the family in any of the various rooms without leaving this desk.[50]

From her "out-of-the-way corner," the housewife could "control" the house without ever leaving her command post. And why should she, when the kitchen was in love with her? Formica's conception of the model house seems quite dated today, but this gender differentiation for an "ideal" prototype reveals that 1964 was closer in social attitudes to 1939 than to 1989.

Probably the most muddle-headed "futuristic" appliance shown at the 1964/65 Fair was a Dish Maker, designed by Walter Dorwin Teague Associates for a

Below: Formica's World's Fair House designed by Emil A. Schmidlin. Advertised as the first home to use Formica on its exterior walls, the interior also featured Formica surfaces throughout. Photograph courtesy of Peter M. Warner.

Below, top and bottom left: The kitchen of Formica's World's Fair House had an indoor barbecue pit. Formica laminate covered all the surfaces. Photographs courtesy of Peter M. Warner and the Rare Books and Manuscripts Division, New York Public Library, Astor, Lenox, and Tilden Foundations.

Below, right: Daughter's room, Formica's World Fair House. Photograph courtesy of the Rare Books and Manuscripts Division, New York Public Library, Astor, Lenox, and Tilden Foundations.

Norge kitchen at the Festival of Gas pavilion. According to a press release from Teague Associates, the Dish Maker produced "new plastic dishes for each meal:"

The number of place settings required were set in the production counter and the machine would injection mold the plates, saucers, cups, and glasses requested. After use, the dirty dishes would be ground into pellets. The pellets would be washed, dried, and returned to the materials hopper for reuse.

It was further claimed that the Dish Maker would conserve space in the kitchen.[51] Not mentioned was that a production unit had simply replaced storage space for dishes, or that it might take longer to operate this machine than to wash old-fashioned china.

In a general architectural sense, there was a great deal of continuity between the 1939/40 and 1964/65 fairs. Several firms designed pavilions for both, including William Lescaze, Skidmore, Owings & Merrill, Kahn & Jacobs, Albert Kahn Associates, Eggers & Higgins; and designers or design firms Henry Dreyfuss, Walter Dorwin Teague Associates, and Donald Deskey Associates. Other firms associated with both fairs were made up of partnerships that differed only slightly from their earlier versions: Voorhees, Walker, Foley & Smith by 1964 had become Voorhees, Walker, Smith, Smith & Haines; Harrison & Fouilhoux was now Harrison & Abramovitz. Nearly all of these firms had become more conservative in their work over the intervening twenty-five years. William Lescaze's tame First National City Bank at the 1964/65 Fair, for example, had none of the pop verve of his Aviation Building in 1939.

Despite outstanding architectural contributions in 1939, such as Alvar Aalto's Finnish pavilion and Oscar Niemeyer and Lucio Costa's Brazilian pavilion, or Saarinen and Eames's IBM pavilion in 1964, neither exposition is in fact remembered for these individual designs. What made the 1939/40 Fair fun and memorable for the public was the care that had gone into its overall conception. What made the 1964/65 Fair less thrilling was Robert Moses's laissez-faire approach to planning, together with the corporate and religious stranglehold he had encouraged. When it became clear that despite all his effort to make money the Fair Corporation was in debt after the first year, Moses relaxed his puritanical stance: sixty-nine new bars were added for the 1965 season, as well as nine discothèques with go-go dancers. But, in the end, this made little difference, for the 1964/65 Fair lost almost as much money as the 1939/40 Fair did.[52]

Outside Kelly & Gruzen's American Express pavilion of 1964 stood a large sculpture, called the *Money Tree.* Its more than six thousand leaves were made up of one million dollars worth of international currency laminated to the branches.[53] Peter Lyon in his *Holiday* essay, "A Glorious Nightmare," had noted the prevalence of artificial trees at the Fair, including the "garden grove" at the IBM pavilion. While the anti-architectural, tree-like forms at the IBM pavilion may remind us of the later sixties, or even of Charles Reich's *The Greening of America* of 1970, it is the large amount of cash laminated into uselessness on the *Money Tree* that provides the best symbolism for the 1964/65 Fair.

Below: The American Express pavilion, designed by Kelly & Gruzen, with "The Money Tree" designed by Samuel Gallo. The tree "sprouted" more than one million dollars worth of currency. Photograph courtesy of Gruzen Samton Steinglass Architects.

Above: Andy Warhol, *Most Wanted Man No. 1, John M.* (front and profile), silkscreen on canvas, two panels, each: 49 × 38⅛ in. Collection of the Herbert F. Johnson Museum of Art, Cornell University; purchase funds from the National Endowment for the Arts and Individual donors. Copyright the Estate and Foundation of Andy Warhol, 1989/ARS NY.

Opposite:
Theodore Roszak, *Forms in Space,* aluminum and stainless steel, height: 38 ft. Photograph by Phyllis Bilick, photography collection of The Queens Museum.

Art for the Millions, or Art for the Market?

Helen A. Harrison

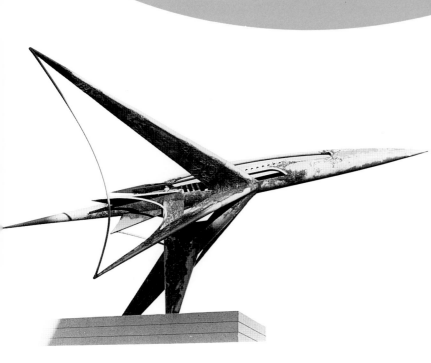

New York City's two twentieth-century international expositions were held at times when American art was undergoing profound changes, particularly in relation to its public. Following six years of government art patronage under various aspects of the New Deal, the 1939/40 New York World's Fair reflected the new art consciousness engendered by mural projects, community art centers, and other activities designed to integrate the arts into daily life. With a philosophical position determined by visions of an ideal future society, the Fair's administration extended the New Deal axiom of "art for the millions" by incorporating art into every aspect of its World of Tomorrow. Its Board of Design planned and executed a massive program of murals and sculpture for the grounds, and its Directors responded favorably to critics who urged them to provide space for exhibitions of both historical and contemporary art.

By 1964, the art world pendulum was on another swing toward populism, having arced back in the direction of elitism during the preceding quarter century. The postwar ascendancy of Abstract Expressionism had been challenged by a younger generation of artists who looked to popular source material in the way that their Depression-era forebears had once found inspiration in the American Scene. Their accessible, audacious, and highly touted efforts—the boosters this time were dealers and the media, rather than the federal government—had opened up new audiences and markets. A world's fair held in New York in 1964/65 might therefore have been expected to capitalize on art's rediscovered popular appeal, and to reflect the shift that had taken place in the national attitude: from one of government responsibility to one of private (i.e., commercial) support for the arts.

It has been said that world's fairs function as "cultural barometers," indicating the relative social, political, economic, and creative pressures that prevail during their eras. By setting the tone for each fair, the administration both responds to these forces and molds public awareness of them, ultimately shaping popular perceptions and reactions. Many people—both inside and outside the governing bodies of the two New York fairs—who understood this chain of cause and effect were eager that art be presented as a vital, integrated element of the expositions.

In 1939, the Fair's theme, "Building the World of Tomorrow," suggested that the overall approach would be visionary, with implications that transcended the temporary nature of the exposition itself. The policy of the federal government, which had established the first of its art patronage programs in 1933, found expression two years later in the recommendations of the Fair of the Future Committee, which prepared the original proposal for a fair reflecting the essential interdependence of all aspects of the American way of life.[1] Acting on this suggestion, the Board of Design noted that "decorative painting, murals and sculpture are necessary in the architectural scheme of the Fair,"[2] and the Committee on Theme directed that "art activities should be closely related to daily life."[3]

As an expression of this concept, the numerous buildings erected by the Fair Corporation for official use or rental by exhibitors were furnished with embellishments commissioned by the Fair, and additional commissions were awarded for sculpture on the grounds. Altogether, more than a hundred painters and sculptors were employed, and many others worked privately for exhibitors, producing a total of 158 murals (some multi-paneled) and 173 sculptures, most of them made expressly for the Fair.[4] The Fair's *Information Manual* proudly noted that "sculpture plays a larger part in the embellishment of the World's Fair grounds than it has at any other exposition."[5] The scale of its decorative program made the Fair arguably the largest short-term public art project ever undertaken.

It seemed to the Fair's Directors and Board of Design that this monumental scheme was sufficient to demonstrate their commitment to integrating art with everyday life. Accordingly, they made no provision for a separate art pavilion, arguing that art was everywhere at the Fair, and that it would be unwise to compete with Manhattan's museums, several of which were planning special exhibitions to coincide with the Fair. The art community, however, exerted

Opposite: The Contemporary Arts Building was renamed the American Art Today Building during the 1940 season of the 1939/40 World's Fair. Designed by Frederick Ackerman, Joshua Lowenfish, and John van Pelt, it housed over 800 works by American artists and rotating exhibits. Photography collection of The Queens Museum.

138

considerable pressure on the Fair's
planners to provide both historical and
contemporary exhibitions, and arguments
in favor of both proposals eventually
prevailed. A structure planned by the Fair
Corporation as a community arts center
was redesignated the Contemporary Arts
Building,[6] financed by the Fair, and
administered by a Governing Committee
of prominent museum officials and artists.[7]
Its 1939 exhibition, "American Art
Today," billed as "the most
representative and democratically selected
exhibition of the work of living American
painters, sculptors and printmakers ever
assembled,"[8] was organized by Holger
Cahill, national director of the Federal Art
Project (FAP) and the Fair's consultant on
contemporary art. During the 1940

season, a similar but smaller show of work from the FAP was held, along with exhibitions organized by such outside groups as the American Abstract Artists and the National Society of Mural Painters.[9]

Responding further to outside pressure, the Fair Corporation approved a proposal for a Fine Arts Building to house an exhibition sponsored by prominent art collectors and dealers. Under the auspices of Art Associates, Inc., a non-profit corporation set up for underwriting purposes, a Masterpieces of Art pavilion designed by Harrison & Fouilhoux was erected. It was decorated with murals by Lyonel Feininger, and filled with 432 works of European art covering the period from the Middle Ages to 1800. Loans came primarily from American collections, but also from museums abroad, including the Louvre, Amsterdam's Rijksmuseum, and the National Gallery in London. Although the Fair Corporation made no financial contribution to the project, it provided a form of subsidy by waiving the building's ground rent. In 1940, the exhibition featured 373 works and, in line with the nationalistic thrust of the "Fortee Fair," included American paintings of the eighteenth and nineteenth centuries; the outbreak of war in Europe prevented the extension of foreign loans.[10]

In addition to the large number of artworks visible on the grounds and within the pavilions, either as part of the architectural ensemble or in special exhibitions, the 1939/40 Fair boasted a broad representation of styles, from academic to avant-garde, and media, both traditional and experimental. The National Society of Mural Painters, dominated by academicians, was out in force, but there were also significant contributions by such leading abstractionists as Stuart Davis, Fernand Léger, and Lyonel Feininger, who also decorated the Fair-sponsored Marine Transportation Building. Younger

painters, including Arshile Gorky and Willem de Kooning, were represented by prominent murals, and FAP sponsorship allowed the inclusion of abstract wall paintings by Ilya Bolotowsky, Balcomb Greene, Byron Browne, and Louis Schanker, as well as an important group of innovative representational murals for the WPA Building.[11]

The Fair's *Information Manual* noted that all outdoor murals, including those of private exhibitors, had been approved by the Board of Design in order to ensure that "every element of building and decoration will blend with and carry out the theme and plan of the Fair."[12] By exercising strong influence over the exterior decorations, the board created a harmonious ensemble that encompassed a diversity of styles, described in a publicity release as "a liberal reflection of the aesthetic forces at work among contemporary artists."[13] At the Contemporary Arts Building, visitors could see a truly representative cross section of current artistic approaches, from the "American Scene" realism of Thomas Hart Benton, John Stuart Curry, and Grant Wood to the non–objective sculpture of David Smith. A program of demonstrations exposed the public to technical processes and stimulated interaction with the artists themselves, encouraging both popular appreciation of and participation in art activity.

An art gallery turned inside out, the fairgrounds complemented the presentations of the specialized pavilions as well as those of corporate and foreign exhibitors which included art in their displays. If contemporary European trends were slighted, this omission only served to highlight the fact that Germany did not participate in the Fair (and even if it had, would not have exhibited the outstanding avant-garde work labeled "decadent" by the Hitler régime), and that the Soviet Union had repudiated its experimental vanguard in favor of the

Below: Murals by Lyonel Feininger in the courtyard of the Masterpieces of Art pavilion, 1939/40 World's Fair. Photograph by T. Lux Feininger. Photography collection of The Queens Museum.

hackneyed Socialist Realism embodied in the giant steel sculpture of an idealized worker that crowned its towering pavilion in 1939.

In planning the art program for the 1964/65 Fair, the administration was mindful of the aims and achievements of its predecessor. Indeed, both fairs shared certain key personnel who contributed to their aesthetic programs. The consultant landscape architect Gilmore D. Clarke, designer of the Unisphere, had been a member of the 1939/40 Fair's Board of Design, while the architect Wallace K. Harrison, a member of the 1964/65 Executive Committee, was a principal in the firm that had designed the Trylon and Perisphere and other pavilions for the World of Tomorrow. Numerous other architects, engineers, and designers, along with several representatives of business and industry, were officially associated in one or another role with both fairs.

Robert Moses, the man who, as New York City Park Commissioner, had imposed his vision of a post-Fair park on the 1939 plan, was now President of the Fair. He viewed the enterprise as the instrument by which he could realize his ultimate goal of creating an immense public recreation ground at the geographical and population center of the city. Although he had written to Harrison in July 1960 that "I should hope we could afford . . . considerable statuary," and asked him to recommend "a few first-rate sculptors here and abroad," Moses also made his personal taste plain: "No freak stabiles and mobiles in the park, I beg you."[14] By October, he had modified the scope of his plan, telling Harrison that, "as to art . . . sponsored and paid for by the Fair, very little of this sort of thing is contemplated."[15] Earlier, he had inquired of Clarke whether the sculptor Paul Manship's four *Moods of Time* figures, installed in a reflecting pool on the 1939/40 Fair's central mall, would be available

for casting in bronze, noting that after the first fair, "we couldn't raise the money to have them cast and they went back to the studio."[16] Evidently, Moses originally had envisioned these works as permanent features of his highly formal public park, and his subsequent directives and executive decisions reflect a decided penchant for the sort of monumental, academic allegory that was Manship's stock in trade.

In the absence of an active Board of Design, which might have conceived a strong, unified artistic program, the 1964/65 Fair administration chose to commission only a few pieces of sculpture as lasting adornments for the grounds-*cum*-park. Despite Harrison's advice to erect the works in temporary form and "make permanent only those pieces of sculpture which turn out to be great works of art,"[17] Moses decided to invite a small group of artists to submit proposals for permanent works; this time, he would get what he wanted with Fair financing at the outset. By limiting his program to a few key pieces, he could guarantee a tangible aesthetic contribution by the Fair to the park environment. However, apart from his predisposition to Manship, Moses did not suggest specific artists for these commissions. He left such delicate matters to an advisory Committee on Sculpture, coordinated by Clarke and composed of the directors of New York's three preeminent museums—James Rorimer of the Metropolitan Museum of Art, René d'Harnoncourt of the Museum of Modern Art, and Thomas Buechner of the Brooklyn Museum. Along with officials of several of the city's other museums, they had already been approached by Louis Ames, the Fair's Director of Cultural Programming, to cooperate in planning special exhibitions coincident with the Fair.[18]

A problem arose almost immediately when, according to Clarke, d'Harnoncourt reacted unfavorably to his

Left: Paul Manship, *Moods of Time—Morning, Day, Evening, Night*—located in Constitution Mall, 1939/40 World's Fair. Photograph by Bob Golby, photography collection of The Queens Museum.

Below: Paul Manship, *Time and the Fates of Man,* located in Constitution Mall, 1939/40 World's Fair. Photograph by Bob Golby, photography collection of The Queens Museum.

design of the Unisphere, which he evidently considered a piece of sculpture. After obligingly providing a list of modern sculptors he believed to be worthy of commissioning—and whom Clarke viewed with undisguised disdain—d'Harnoncourt decided not to associate himself with the Fair.[19]

With Rorimer and Buechner representing less vanguard sensibilities, the committee endorsed Moses's plan for a few major commissions, recommending "that we should have a range of sculpture from contemporary conservative to the more conservative avant-garde." In Clarke's view, this would ensure that "there should be something to please— no, not everyone—a majority, possibly."[20] The committee's short list of recommended sculptors, issued in May 1961, included ten modernists: Theodore Roszak, Seymour Lipton, David Smith, Herbert Ferber, Isamu Noguchi, Richard Lippold, David Hare, José de Rivera, Ibram Lassaw, and, no doubt to the chagrin of Moses and Clarke, Alexander Calder, perpetrator of the "freak stabiles and mobiles" so abhorrent to them both. From the ranks of the academicians, the committee suggested Robert Foster, Marshall Fredericks, and Paul Manship, all veterans of the 1939/40 Fair.[21]

The Fair's most prestigious commission ironically went to a sculptor the committee had not initially recommended. As early as November 1959, even before Moses had been appointed as President of the Fair, Donald De Lue wrote offering his services "to help protect the Fair from artistic desecration and being an insult to the American people."[22] Later, De Lue prepared sketches on the theme of man's flight into space, which the sculpture committee considered a month after filing its recommendations. However, even the conservative Clarke had reservations. "I do not think of this as a permanent piece," he wrote, "but rather [as] one

Opposite: Donald De Lue, *The Rocket Thrower,* bronze, height: 45 ft. At the close of the Fair, this sculpture remained in Flushing Meadow Park. Photograph by Phyllis Bilick, photography collection of The Queens Museum.

Right: Marshall Fredericks, *Freedom of the Human Spirit,* bronze, height: 24 ft. Photograph by Phyllis Bilick, photography collection of The Queens Museum.

Below: Paul Manship, *Armillary Sphere and Sundial,* bronze, diameter: 10 ft. Photograph courtesy of the Rare Books and Manuscripts Division, New York Public Library, Astor, Lenox, and Tilden Foundations.

done in plaster and gilded for the duration of the Fair."[23]

On November 24, 1961, the Committee on Sculpture made its final recommendations for five commissions, based on plaster models submitted by the artists. Manship offered a ten-foot armillary sphere, designed for another project and ready for casting in bronze. De Lue's maquette of a symbolic figure was also approved, as was de Rivera's proposal for a free-form steel sculpture. Fredericks's design required additional development, the committee reported, but tentative approval was given. The committee rejected the proposals of Foster and Lippold, noted that Noguchi had never replied to their invitation, and suggested that Calder be asked to take his place.[24]

To what must have been Moses's relief, Calder declined the invitation. The second artist on the list of recommendations was Roszak, who submitted sketches for a semi-abstract sculpture on the theme of transportation. The forward thrust of his *Forms in Space,* forty-two feet long and executed in aluminum over stainless steel, evoked the progressive development of movement, from natural means of human locomotion and the motion of aquatic and airborne creatures to the technological dynamics of the airplane, submarine, and rocket.[25] Sited near the Hall of Science, adjacent to the Space Park, it complemented the theme of the surrounding exhibits with an appropriately metaphorical response to the concept of man's aspiration toward space travel.

De Lue's solution to a similar hypothesis was more allegorical. His piece, *The Rocket Thrower,* was a heroic male embodiment of motive power. Occupying the most prominent location on the Fair's principal axis, the forty-three-foot bronze dominated the central mall. The stylized, discreetly draped figure balanced on an ascending curve of metal as he reached toward a constellation of gilded stars. From his right hand issued a comet-like form rising above the stars and into the heavens. In De Lue's interpretation, the conquest of space is not a technological victory, but a mythological phenomenon.

Needless to say, *The Rocket Thrower* was greeted with less than universal acclaim by New York's art tastemakers. The most outspoken denunciation came from John Canaday, chief critic of the *New York Times,* who characterized it as "the most lamentable monster" on view, "an absurdity that might be a satire of the kind of sculpture already discredited at the time of the 1939 fair."[26] Predictably, De Lue dismissed the critique. He wrote to Moses that "the intemperance of [Canaday's] comments is an indication, I believe, of fear and frustration," crowing that it was going to be hard for the critic and his "pals . . . to tout this poverty-stricken and stupid abstract sculpture with the Rocket Thrower so much in evidence."[27] Moses replied: "Those whose opinion *[sic]* I respect like your contribution. It will be conspicuous long after the Canadays are forgotten."[28] Never one to shrink from defending his projects, Moses in this case fell back on the judgment of others and remained outside the debate on the sculpture's merits. Yet, as the focal point of his post-Fair park, *The Rocket Thrower* has become a monument to his vision and a symbol of his taste.

Without involving himself openly in the aesthetic issues that governed the commissions for sculpture in his park, Moses nevertheless exerted considerable influence by enlisting Clarke as his de facto agent. The two men had had a close professional relationship since the mid-1920s, when Clarke had been the landscape architect for the Bronx River Parkway. He had also served as Moses's spokesman on the design of the 1939/40

Fair, ensuring the radial layout upon which Moses could realize his concept of a formal recreation ground. Thus, of the five commissions offered for permanent sculptures, the three most prominent went to artists whose work sat firmly within the academic tradition. Indeed, Marshall Fredericks, the only one of the five sculptors still living, believes it was Clarke who recommended him for the commission, and who was the likely champion of De Lue's work to the sculpture committee.[29]

Roszak's piece, semi-abstract but easily recognizable as an evocation of the transportation theme, was relegated to a lesser site on the Fair's (therefore the park's) periphery. De Rivera's *Free Form* was a slender stainless steel curve of modest dimensions, with a total height, including a nine-foot polished granite base, of less than twenty feet. Its placement near the New York City Building afforded an attractive but secondary prospect, unlike the unimpeded vistas created for *The Rocket Thrower,* for Manship's sphere, located in its own landscaped setting just west of the Unisphere, and for Fredericks's twenty-four-foot bronze, *Freedom of the Human Spirit,* at the north end of the Court of States. Less allegorical than De Lue's *Rocket Thrower,* it embodied the free spirit in two figures, male and female, ascending skyward in the company of flying swans—a latter-day Adam and Eve returned to the state of grace they enjoyed before the Fall.

Contrary to published reports of the Fair's art program as limited to these few commissions, there was also a plan—unfortunately unrealized—for an exhibition of modern sculpture under Fair sponsorship. The idea was apparently proposed by Judge Samuel I. Rosenman, a longtime Moses associate and member of the Fair's Executive Committee,[30] and it was backed, although not officially recommended, by the Committee on Sculpture. The original proposal was

José de Rivera, *Free Form,* bronze and granite, height: 18 ft. Photograph by Phyllis Bilick, photography collection of The Queens Museum.

rather vague, involving the loan of works by well-known European sculptors—among them Henry Moore, Alberto Giacometti, Jean Arp, Marino Marini, and Ossip Zadkine—as well as by several prominent Americans, for installation somewhere on the grounds. Moses greeted the plan with skepticism. "It is too long a list," he told Stuart Constable, Vice President for Operations, "and everything looks better at first blush than it does after consideration." Conceding that "there may be places where we could use some things of this sort," he suggested, in deference to Rosenman, that "we might, of course, have a Court of Modern Sculpture."[31]

Throughout 1962, plans for the exhibition proceeded fitfully. In spite of Moses's reminder to Constable that "our limited statuary program has been definitely decided," he apparently was willing reluctantly to commit up to $200,000 of Fair money to a sculpture garden in order to appease "the enthusiasts for modern stuff who have offered to loan objects."[32] Plans were drawn, but when Constable reported that the proposed architect, I. Ming Pei, had estimated the cost of landscaping and installation at "well over $300,000," and that the total cost of the exhibition, not counting operation, would exceed half a million dollars, Rosenman advised that "we should consider the matter dead." "Right," replied Moses with relief. "Thank God that spasm is over."[33]

In fact, in matters of sculpture, Moses's attention was primarily directed to two other projects: negotiations with the Vatican involving the display of a selection of its art treasures; and persuading Joseph Hirshhorn to install his renowned sculpture collection at the Fair, with a view to making the pavilion a permanent feature of the park. Far more impressed by and sympathetic to pedigreed art by acknowledged masters, Moses responded enthusiastically to proposals involving such material. In reply to a suggestion by Ames that they negotiate with Dr. Albert Barnes to bring his famous and virtually inaccessible collection from his private museum in Merion, Pennsylvania to a New York City museum or even to the fairgrounds, Moses wrote, "this is the sort of stuff we want."[34]

When the unprecedented and controversial agreement with the Vatican was completed, Moses could justifiably claim much of the credit for persuading Pope John XXIII to exhibit Michelangelo's *Pietà* (installed in Old St. Peter's Basilica in 1499 and never before removed from the Vatican), among other art treasures. The progress of the negotiations, which Moses conducted personally with His Holiness, and the subsequent debate over the wisdom of transporting the 465-year-old marble sculpture to and from the Fair, were avidly reported in the press, as were Moses's successful efforts to persuade the government of Spain to send masterpieces by Goya, Velázquez, and El Greco that made that country's building one of the highlights of the Fair.

The Moses negotiations with Hirshhorn proved less effective. On learning that the industrialist was actively searching for a permanent home for his collection, with its major representation of European sculpture, Moses offered to provide a museum site on the fairgrounds. He even went as far as having plans drawn up, and conducted Hirshhorn on a private tour, ferrying him to the grounds by helicopter and showering him with the charm and attention he had often applied so effectively to others.

In spite of these blandishments, Hirshhorn was not to be dissuaded from seeking a more glamorous venue for his collection. In October 1962, he wrote to Moses that "no matter how enticing your proposal is and I must admit it is quite generous, the idea of creating my museum in the borough of Queens does

Below, top: Delivery of the *Pietà* to the Vatican Pavilion. Photograph

Below, bottom: Aerial view of the Vatican pavilion designed by York & Sawyer, Hurley & Hughes, and Luder & Associates. Photograph courtesy of Peter M. Warner.

Opposite: Michelangelo, *Pietà* in the Vatican pavilion, installation by theatrical designer Jo Mielziner. Viewers traveled past the statue on a moving sidewalk. Estate of Jo Mielziner. Photograph courtesy of Peter M. Warner.

not strike a responsive note." He was actively pursuing an alternative location in Manhattan, he said.[35] Infuriated by Hirshhorn's attitude, Moses nevertheless pursued him. As late as the winter of 1964–65, after the close of the Fair's first season, he wrote to his staff that "Mr. Joseph Hirshhorn may be back with some of his collection" and outlined plans for an outdoor sculpture garden.[36] This time, Hirshhorn sent his curator, Abram Lerner, to inspect the proposed site. In Lerner's view, the idea was unacceptable. "They were going to put us in between some commercial enterprise and something else—it would have destroyed the whole significance of the collection," he says. After two and a half years of enduring what he described as "the antics of . . . the demon art collector," Moses abandoned his pursuit of the elusive Hirshhorn.[37]

Moses's appeals to prospective sponsors aside, it was the requirement of sponsorship itself—his insistence that, apart from the five official commissions and the abortive modern sculpture exhibition, all installations or exhibitions must be privately financed—that mitigated against a significant role for art at the Fair. Proposal after proposal submitted by outside interests fell through when foundation or corporate support failed to materialize. Even Hirshhorn, however ardently he was being wooed, would have been required to pay for the museum building Moses had offered him, and to finance its operation. The Fair, Moses declared, was not in the business of sponsoring art.

This position was roundly condemned by the editors and editorial board of *Art in America,* one of the country's leading art magazines. In a letter to Moses, also released to the press, they expressed concern that the Fair's attitude toward art "would serve to confirm the frequent criticism of our country as an entirely materialistic

nation."[38] Similar concerns had also been troubling Lloyd Goodrich, director of the Whitney Museum, who recalled the important contribution made by the Contemporary Arts Building to the 1939/40 Fair. Along with other influential members of the New York art community, Goodrich believed that supplementary exhibitions in the city's museums still would not "fulfill the purposes of an outstanding art exhibition in the Fair itself."[39]

Among the various proposals submitted for art pavilions was one by Evelyn Sharp, a retired hotel magnate, who suggested a building devoted to contemporary art from distinguished private collections; she withdrew when her plan to establish a $1.5 million private foundation to finance the scheme fell through.[40] Grant Smith and Associates, a New York marketing firm, drew up a detailed prospectus for "The World of Fine Art," to comprise an international selection of art treasures, but it also folded when the required sponsorship (this time corporate) failed to materialize.[41] And when the American Federation of Arts wrote to offer its services in organizing a Fair-sponsored exhibition, Constable—who had yet to be saddled with the modern sculpture proposal—replied that "the Fair Corporation does not propose to have an Art Exhibit at the Fair Grounds."[42]

The most actively promoted plan involved a reincarnation of the 1939 Contemporary Arts Building. A coalition calling itself the Committee of Artists' Societies, representing fourteen groups as diverse as the Audubon Society and the Society of Abstract Artists, proposed a pavilion of aluminum and rubberized plastic sections, designed by the architect August Sak and intended to remain after the Fair as a permanent museum for the borough of Queens.[43] The committee's chairman, cartoonist and muralist Hugo Gellert, had been active in persuading the

Opposite: The opening of the exhibition, "American Art To-Day," in the Pavilion of Fine Arts. Shown (left to right): president of the pavilion, Norman E. Blankman, next to a painting by Jimmy Ernst; Chief Justice Earl Warren; playwright Arthur Miller; Senator Kenneth Keating; and conductor Leopold Stokowski. Works by 250 American artists were on display. Photograph courtesy of the Rare Books and Manuscripts Division, New York Public Library, Astor, Lenox, and Tilden Foundations.

Above: Pavilion of Fine Arts. Designed by Paul K. Y. Chen as Argentina's pavilion, it was taken over by the Long Island Arts Center. Photograph courtesy of the Rare Books and Manuscripts Division, New York Public Library, Astor, Lenox, and Tilden Foundations.

Below: Interior of the Spanish pavilion showing the painting exhibition; left: Goya, *La Maja Vestida;* right: Velázquez, *Pabillo.* Photography courtesy of The Queens Borough Public Library, Long Island Division.

administration of the earlier Fair to sponsor the "American Art Today" exhibition in the Contemporary Art Building, and his new proposal was substantially similar.

Taking his case to the press, Gellert approached Emily Genauer, the art critic of the New York *Herald Tribune,* to whom he handed what she assumed was a press release describing efforts to get the Fair to sponsor a contemporary art exhibition. To her amusement, what Genauer found herself reading was her own 1938 article protesting the decision to exclude formal exhibitions from the World of Tomorrow. "If you want to see an art show," she had written, then ". . . you must leave this great exposition of everything important in contemporary American life and go eight miles away to the Metropolitan." Voicing hope that the 1963 lobbying effort would be as successful as its predecessor, she noted that "absolutely nothing has changed in twenty-five years."[44]

On that score, she was mistaken. Unlike Grover Whalen and the Directors of the 1939/40 Fair, Moses and his administration were not to be swayed. The most they would offer was a site on the grounds, providing that outside sponsorship was forthcoming. At a press conference, Gellert declared that the plan was doomed unless "some individual or foundation [were] to come forward and cover themselves with glory."[45]

In the spring, with the Fair's opening approaching and no financing for the project forthcoming, *Art News* magazine dubbed Moses the "Art Slayer" whose Fair "combines the tone of a carney shill with the spirit of a black-marketeer." Thomas B. Hess's editorial took note of art shows planned by various exhibitors, but considered these efforts insufficient antidotes to the policy that made a mockery of the Fair's pledge to display "the finest products of the spirit, mind and hand" of man. He recalled that

it was the then City Park Commissioner who had demolished the 1939/40 Fair's Masterpieces of Art Building, which its sponsors had offered to the city as a permanent art museum.[46]

In fact, eleventh-hour efforts by a group calling itself the Long Island Arts Center, Inc. were successful in providing sponsorship for a contemporary exhibition. Space fortuitously became available when the government of Argentina withdrew support for its pavilion, leaving the building without a tenant. The arts center group, dominated by prominent Long Island businessmen, saw the Fair as an opportunity to demonstrate credibility for a Nassau County art museum which it was in the process of planning.[47] Although the Fair had opened a month earlier, the scheme was deemed feasible, since the Committee of Artists' Societies' exhibition was fully developed and required only a suitable venue and sufficient financing. In mid-May 1964, the two groups came to an agreement with the Fair, and the Argentine building became the Pavilion of Fine Arts.

The exhibition was less comprehensive and less favorably received than had been its 1939 counterpart. Instead of the 1500 pieces Gellert and his group had originally envisioned, it contained only 150 paintings, 50 pieces of sculpture, and 50 prints, purporting to represent, in the words of the Whitney's Lloyd Goodrich, a member of the advisory committee, "the whole picture of American art today."[48] The critics did not share his enthusiasm. Canaday declared that it had "emerged stillborn" from the protracted labor it had required. "Not many of the artists are represented by their top works," he wrote, citing important omissions and dubious inclusions.[49] He described the show as "a virtuous assemblage of good, goodish, weak and paltry" examples making up an "unfocused collection of

Left: Allan D'Arcangelo, *Transportation,* mural on the exterior of the Transportation and Travel pavilion. 27 × 20 ft. Photograph by Peter M. Warner.

Below: Allan D'Arcangelo, *Undersea Life,* mural on the exterior of the Transportation and Travel pavilion. D'Arcangelo did three murals for the building, the third entitled, *First Landing on the Moon.* Photograph courtesy of Photofest.

unclassified merchandise arranged in unexplained juxtapositions."[50] "The best that can be said for the show is that it really did happen," wrote Charlotte Willard of the New York *Post,* reiterating Canaday's critique.[51] Genauer of the *Herald Tribune* dissented, praising "both the variety and compatibility of the works presented."[52]

The pavilion's late opening prevented it from being listed in the Fair's *Official Guide,* so even purposeful visitors undaunted by negative reviews had a hard time finding the exhibition. Phyllis Braff, the curator who handled the operational aspects of the show, recalls that most of those who came "just wandered in."[53] By mid-July, poor attendance forced its cancellation. A new exhibition, "Mother and Child in Modern Art," organized by the American Federation of Arts and sponsored by Clairol, was brought from the Time-Life Building in Manhattan and opened in the pavilion in mid-August. Despite modest success, with a reduced admission charge and as many as 500 visitors a day reported in the press,[54] the building was operating heavily in the red and failed to reopen in 1965.

During the Fair's second season, contemporary American art was represented by "Art '65," an exhibition of paintings and sculpture by fifty-nine lesser-known and unknown artists, selected by Brian O'Doherty, editor of *Show* magazine, and art historian Wayne Andersen of M.I.T. for the American Express pavilion, where the "Money Tree" was the principal attraction. Writing in *Studio International,* Dore Ashton described the show in negative terms similar to those applied to "American Art To-Day," but congratulated the organizers for "render[ing] us a service, no matter how inadequately," by including the work of West Coast artists not previously seen in the East. However, she also noted the troubling appearance of censorship when, "after making grand statements of their

sober duty in presenting the work . . . without prejudice, American Express took fright and withdrew some eight paintings selected by O'Doherty." In Ashton's view, corporate sponsorship meant that "commercial motives of a big company inevitably intervene and dignity flies out the window."[55]

For the most part, however, those art exhibitions incorporated into larger displays, where they could capitalize on general attendance, fared better than the Pavilion of Fine Arts in terms of both visitors and critical reception. There was universal acclaim for Spain's outstanding selection of canvases by old and modern masters, crowned by Goya's naked and clothed Majas, along with contemporary works by Picasso and Miró. "The World of Ancient Gold" in the Transportation and Travel pavilion boasted a dramatic installation by Philip Johnson and offered "one of the very few coherent presentations at this Fair," according to *Art News.*[56] And Canaday praised "Four Centuries of American Art," in the Better Living Center, as "closer to being a summary than you would think so small a show could be." Impressed by the high quality of the forty-one paintings and five sculptures, ranging from a seventeenth-century anonymous portrait through examples by Copley, Sargent, Sloan, de Kooning, and Pollock, Canaday described the ensemble as "selected with such discernment that this minor exhibition becomes a major pleasure." But he protested that, in general, even outstanding smaller shows were upstaged by the welter of surrounding material. "They are worth seeing," he concluded, "but to get there, and out again, without suffering spiritual and esthetic offense on the way, is impossible."[57]

It was in fact Canaday's contention that art exhibitions at the Fair were a waste of time. When Moses came out against the plan for a contemporary art pavilion, Canaday alone defended the

Right: *Electronia,* by Kenneth Snelson, being airlifted to the Fair. Constructed of suspended aluminum tubes, the piece measured 30 × 35 ft., and adorned the entrance of the Tower of Light pavilion. Photograph courtesy of Peter M. Warner.

Below: Night view of the Tower of Light pavilion designed by Synergetics, Inc. A Kenneth Snelson sculpture was installed at the entrance. Photograph courtesy of Photofest.

decision in print. Under the headline "Pardon The Heresy," he dissented from the majority view that an art exhibition is an essential ingredient of any fair when he wrote that one "isolated within this vast midway, would not even be an effective counter-irritant," advising that the only appropriate art pavilion "would have to be one where dealers could rent space and hawk their wares."[58] His argument that "contemporary art properly belongs incorporated within contemporary life" was most sympathetic to those pavilions that integrated art and architecture, such as Japan's sculpted stone wall by Masayuki Nagare, which he dubbed "the finest single work of art created for the Fair."[59] Other laudable efforts in this vein included the Transportation and Travel building's wraparound "supergraphic" mural of road, water, and space motifs by Allan D'Arcangelo; the Electric Light and Power Company's Tower of Light, with its two stainless steel and aluminum sculptures, titled *Electronia,* by Kenneth Snelson; and Philip Johnson's New York State Building, for which the architect had commissioned exterior murals and sculpture by ten contemporary artists. "The art will probably be flashy," Canaday predicted, "but . . . as contemporary art it will probably make more sense to people for being incorporated architecturally instead of hanging on display independently."[60]

The New York State building commissions included works by leading artists of the younger generation—the oldest, Alexander Liberman, was fifty-one; the youngest, James Rosenquist, was thirty. The group included Pop artists Roy Lichtenstein, Andy Warhol, Robert Indiana, Robert Rauschenberg, and Rosenquist, hard-edge abstractionists Ellsworth Kelly and Liberman, and sculptors Peter Agostini, John Chamberlain, and Robert Mallary. Their works were hung on the outside of the pavilion's cylindrical "Theaterama."

Below: Andy Warhol, *Thirteen Most Wanted Men*, silkscreen on canvas, 20 × 20 ft. Installed on the exterior of the New York State pavilion, the mural consisted of enlarged "mug shots," described by Philip Johnson as, "A comment on the sociological factor of American life." Photograph courtesy of UPI/Bettmann Newsphotos. Copyright the Estate and Foundation of Andy Warhol, 1989/ARS New York.

Warhol's mural, *Thirteen Most Wanted Men*, made up of screenprinted enlargements of FBI wanted posters, was the only piece to provoke controversy, and even then, the furor was confined to the Fair's inner circle. The full-face and profile mug shots of fugitives, screened onto forty-eight-inch-square canvases, were mounted on the building in mid-April, but within a few days they were painted over and subsequently removed. Although the press reported simply that the removal was requested by Warhol because he was "displeased with the work's effect," Johnson later gave a different explanation: "The names [of the subjects] got to Governor Rockefeller; [the men] were all Italian. . . . Most of these 'Thirteen Wanted' were Mafiosi." In spite of having described them as Mafia members, Johnson also claimed that many of the men on the list had already been "proved not guilty." Identifying them as wanted criminals would therefore have subjected him, the artist, and the state to "lawsuits from here to the end of the world," he explained. Thus the mural was removed for political rather than aesthetic reasons. Not to be daunted, Warhol proposed to substitute a portrait of Moses—a suggestion vetoed by Johnson as in bad taste. "I forbade that," he said, "because I just don't think it made any sense to thumb our noses. . . . Andy and I had a little battle at the time, although he is one of my favorite artists."[61]

The works of the remaining painters were all Pop in style, with Lichtenstein's untitled deadpan quotation of a comic-strip woman leaning out a window setting an irreverent tone followed throughout the ensemble. Both Rosenquist and Rauschenberg, taking their imagery from a variety of mass-media sources, produced montages commenting on the American fascination with food, technology, progress, and the space race. The centerpiece of Rosenquist's untitled twenty-foot panel is

Below, top: The Warhol mural, deemed too controversial by Governor Rockefeller, was whitewashed over but the images could still be seen. It was subsequently covered with black cloth and eventually removed. Photograph by Peter M. Warner.

Below, bottom: Andy Warhol, *Robert Moses,* silkscreen on canvas. Warhol proposed that panels of this portrait of Moses replace the *Thirteen Most Wanted Men* mural. Philip Johnson thought the work was in bad taste and rejected the proposition.

Photography by Shunk-Kender, courtesy of Leo Castelli Gallery. Copyright the Estate and Foundation of Andy Warhol, 1989/ARS New York.

Below: Alexander Liberman, *Prometheus,* painted aluminum, 20 × 20 ft. Collection of the University Art Museum, University of Minnesota, gift of the artist. Photograph courtesy of Jim Strong.

Opposite, top left: Roy Lichtenstein, *World's Fair Mural,* oil on plywood, 20 × 16 ft. Collection of the University Art Museum, University of Minnesota, gift of the artist. Photograph courtesy of Jim Strong. © Roy Lichtenstein/VAGA New York 1988.

Opposite, top right: James Rosenquist, *World's Fair Mural,* oil on masonite, 20 × 20 ft. Collection of the University Art Museum, University of Minnesota, gift of the artist. Photograph courtesy of Jim Strong. © James Rosenquist/VAGA New York 1988.

Opposite, below: Robert Indiana, *E.A.T.* The Liberman, Lichtenstein, Indiana, and Rosenquist works were installed on the exterior of the New York State pavilion, designed by Philip Johnson. Photograph by Gert Berliner.

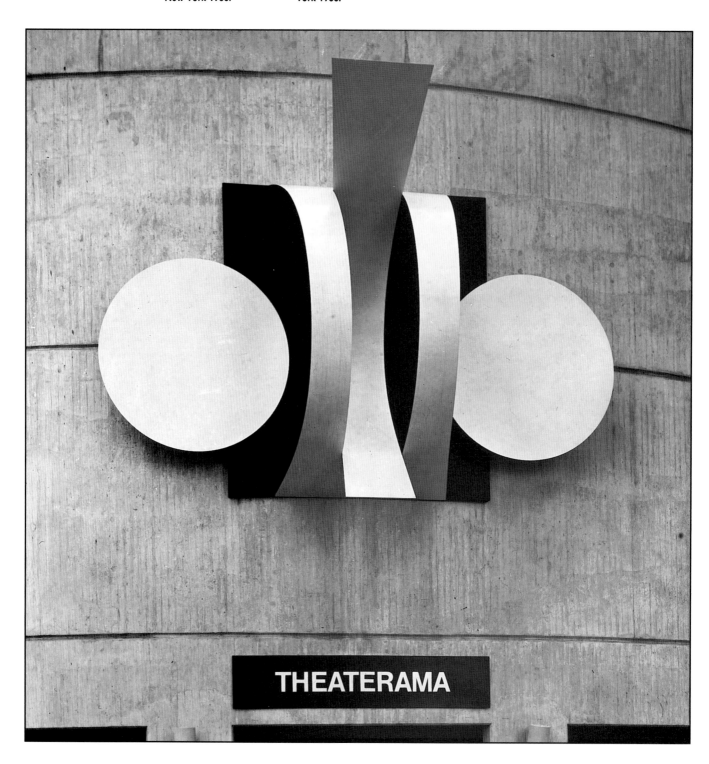

THEATERAMA

Uncle Sam's top hat, its stripes humorously echoing those on a straw protruding from the mouth of a Coke bottle. In *Skyway,* Rauschenberg's most poignant icon is a news photo of the late President Kennedy, whose assassination a brief five months before the Fair's opening was still a raw wound in the American consciousness.

In sculpture, the works ranged from the cool, clean geometry of Kelly's painted aluminum relief, *Two Curves: Blue Red,* and Liberman's *Prometheus,* a structure of concave, convex, and circular aluminum sheets, to Chamberlain's baroque assemblage of crushed car parts, Agostini's *A Windy Autumn Day*—ghostly plaster versions of balloons and tarpaulins floating along the concrete wall—and Mallary's frieze of resin-covered tailcoats, *The Cliffhanger,* suspended in space like charred human figures frozen in a failed attempt at escape. Indiana's marquee-like sign, blinking the letters "E-A-T," commented wryly on modern voracity, implying that art is just another consumable product.

The works failed to provoke the outrage that some observers had anticipated. By 1964, hybrid sculpture that adopted the coloration and formal vocabulary of painting was already commonplace, and Pop Art had moved from a vanguard position to one of solid acceptance, not only by the elite but also on a far broader level of popular appeal. With a new breed of dealers, curators, and collectors actively promoting the younger generation, and in spite of the reservations and even open hostility expressed in the art press, admiring articles appeared in mass-market publications such as *Time, Newsweek, Life, Vogue,* and the *Ladies Home Journal.*[62] The art on the New York State Building's exterior served collectively as a kind of aesthetic billboard, advertising the up-to-date tastes of its architect and the state's Governor, Nelson A. Rockefeller,

Below: John Chamberlain, *Untitled,* painted and chrominum-plated steel, dimensions unknown. Photograph courtesy of Jim Strong.

Below: Robert Mallary, *The Cliffhanger*, wood, cloth and plastic. Photograph courtesy of Jim Strong.

and announcing that New York was to be identified with the very latest trends in painting and sculpture.

In contrast, the interior exhibition, "Art in New York State," included landscape paintings and portraits of the eighteenth and nineteenth centuries, demonstrating that the state had a rich artistic heritage, albeit one that relied heavily on European precedents. Outside, it was clear that the "art market" had supplanted the "art world" as the force to be reckoned with in contemporary cultural development. As a reflection of this trend, the exterior of the New York State Building's rotunda accorded nicely with the consumer-oriented tone of the Fair as a whole, a subtle irony that was probably not apparent to Moses. Only the apocalyptic character of Mallary's anguished forms, harking back to the expressionistic, semi-abstract figures created by Pollock and de Kooning twenty years earlier, overtly expressed the decadence implicit in the other works.

At the opposite extreme from New York's materialistic approach to art, the Vatican pavilion aimed to popularize the spiritual. The *Pietà,* displayed in a setting by Broadway stage designer Jo Mielziner, was seen through a plexiglas security shield from a series of viewing tiers, moving platforms affording about a minute's glimpse of Michelangelo's early masterpiece. While no commentator questioned the sculpture's status as a major work of art, many criticized the installation, with its dramatic lighting and canned music, as overly theatrical, even kitschy. *Art News* complained that the piece was presented "amid Gregorian Muzak, under flickering blue lights which turn the creamy marble to sugary white."[63] The result was an overwrought pseudospirituality that debased the work's aesthetic qualities even as it strove to heighten the impact of the tableau. The present writer, observing the spectacle from the lowest tier, noted that the floor

Below, top: Peter Agostini, *A Windy Autumn Day,* plaster, 10 × 15 ft. Collection of the University Art Museum, University of Minnesota, gift of the artist. Photograph courtesy of Jim Strong.

Below, bottom: Robert Rauschenberg, *Skyway,* oil and silkscreen on canvas, 18 × 16 ft. Collection of the Dallas Museum of Art, purchase the Roberta Coke Camp Fund, the 500 Inc., Mr. & Mrs. Mark Shepherd Jr., and the General Acquisition Fund. The Agostini and Rauschenberg

works were exhibited on the exterior of the New York State pavilion. Photograph courtesy of Jim Strong.
© Robert Rauschenberg/ VAGA New York 1988.

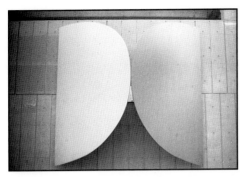

Left and below: Ellsworth Kelly, *Two Curves: Blue Red,* painted aluminum; 18 × 18 ft. Collection of the President and Fellows of Harvard College, gift of the artist. Shown during installation. Photographs by the artist. © Ellsworth Kelly/VAGA New York 1988.

below was littered with piles of discarded film boxes and wrappers, reinforcing the impression that the experience was for many visitors less a spiritual awakening than a "photo opportunity."

The dubious distinction of the most controversial work at the Fair was reserved for a painting of little artistic merit but significant political potential. In an exposition that purported to celebrate "Peace Through Understanding," the furor it aroused severely tested a premise already damaged by perceptions of the Fair as a monument to commerce. And, in a twist of fate that no doubt amused his art-world critics, it cast Robert Moses in an unlikely role, as the defender of freedom of expression.

The controversy erupted following the dedication of the Jordan pavilion. Inside the building, where fragments of a Dead Sea scroll were to have been the most prominent exhibit, a mural traced the history of the Palestinian people. It culminated in a portrait of a mother and child appealing to the world to aid the refugees who, according to an inscription, had been driven from their land by "strangers from abroad" who were threatening to "make the desert bloom with warriors." Although the accusation was unspecific, the implication was clear. Officials of the American-Israel pavilion demanded that the Fair "take immediate action to correct this situation," charging that the mural violated a regulation prohibiting propaganda by one nation against another. "All pavilions are propaganda," replied an official of Jordan, asserting that "we are not against the Jews, but we are against Israel and the foreigners who took over our homes and property."[64]

The dispute escalated when twelve members of the American Jewish Congress were arrested on Moses's orders for picketing the Jordan pavilion. In spite of a court order threatening to revoke the Fair's charter, and a City Council resolution demanding the mural's removal, Moses stood firm against what he termed "suppression of free speech." He pointed out that the American-Israel pavilion had been allowed to erect a critical parody of the mural designed to counter Jordan's attack, and that both pro-Arab and pro-Israel factions were distributing leaflets supporting their positions.[65] Moses's actions in defense of the mural were hardly signs of his support for the First Amendment, but illustrated an attitude that tolerated nothing less than approbation for his work.

It is paradoxical that Moses's need for absolute control over all aspects of his enterprise should have resulted in the free-for-all "Laissez Fair" scored by critics for its lack of aesthetic integrity. In Grover Whalen's 1939/40 Fair, art was one of the major ingredients that welded its disparate elements into a unified whole. By committing substantial resources to an art program, by relinquishing control of that program to a strong Board of Design, and by heeding the advice of cultural leaders, Whalen enabled his World of Tomorrow to express its idealistic concepts by way of a well-coordinated artistic strategy. Yet it should be remembered that Whalen's fair embodied the ideal future, not the real one. The wide-ranging program of public art that had been so vigorously nurtured during the New Deal was killed by a Congress eager to divert relief funds to rearmament, and the America that emerged in the postwar years no longer embraced the concept of "art for the millions"—at least not at public expense. In the twenty-five years between the fairs, American art entered the marketplace as never before. If that fact was reflected with a vengeance in 1964/65, then Moses's fair, with its emphasis on private enterprise, may have been a more accurate "cultural barometer" than we would like to admit.

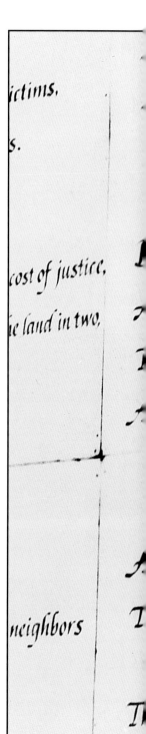

Below: Detail of the mural in the Jordan pavilion which sparked controversy, particularly with the neighboring American-Israel pavilion. The mural traced the history of the Palestinian people and culminated with a portrait of a refugee mother and child, driven from their homeland by "strangers from abroad." Photograph courtesy of The Queens Borough Public Library, Long Island Division.

lives in exile

to go home.

now, to protect their gains ill-got.

land was theirs and had the right,

reatening to disturb the Jordan's course

e the desert bloom with warriors.

o's to stop them?

d seems not to care.

is blinded still.

hy I'm glad you stopped

1964 World's Fair scarf.
Collection of The Queens
Museum, purchase.
Photograph by Jim Strong,
courtesy of The Queens
Museum.

Icons and Images: The Cultural Legacy of the 1964/65 World's Fair

Ileen Sheppard

Indisputably, world's fairs have a strong impact on the popular imagination; anybody who has attended one has a story to relate about the experience. Created as temporary cultural and technological tours de force, the fairs leave us with a lasting impression composed of personal remembrances that are fueled by a tangible material legacy of souvenirs, photographs, and works of art. What's more, the scientific and artistic inventiveness that debuts at these events often has a broad impact on society as a whole. Much of this is derived from the fact that fairs are cultural common denominators that cut across social and class distinctions. They become shared experiences among diverse groups of people. In his article, "Technology as

Theme Park: A Nutshell History of World's Fairs," George Melrod observes: "The World's Fair was 'civilized' entertainment, yes! but behind the 'intellectual' reward of reaping knowledge was the more basic satisfaction of participating in a vast public celebration, milling amid unknown splendor, breathing in the excitement of the spirit of the age."[1]

The time in a person's life when a fair is experienced has as much to do with the memory of the event as the event itself. For the members of the baby-boom generation—people born in the late 1940s and early 1950s—the 1964 World's Fair was a very potent force in their development. Whether they remember having their first beer in the Lowenbrau Beer Garden, meeting members of the opposite sex on the fairgrounds, seeing technological wonders, or undergoing dozens of other coming-of-age experiences while visiting the Fair—on their own, with their families, or on a school trip—the event has permeated the memory of an entire generation.

For many, the Fair remembrance is inextricably linked to the experience of seeing New York for the first time. For youngsters or teenagers, the 1964/65 Fair offered a peek at what the future had in store and displayed apparently limitless vistas into the present world. At the Fair, one had the opportunity to journey around the world and through space as well as to explore new art and technologies. The crass commercialism so frequently touted by the Fair's critics does not taint the collective memory of the baby boomers. Peter Lyons in *Holiday* put it aptly:

I am aware of the many complaints about the Fair. It is too commercial; too little space has been set aside for the fine arts, and almost none for the performing arts; few European countries are officially represented; there is no architectural unity; triviality and vulgarity abound. Most of these charges are true; none of them matters. The salient fact is that the New York World's Fair 1964–1965 is a splendid concentrate of magic and malarkey, well worth seeing despite the crowds, the frustrations, the long queues and even horrifying price.[2]

Right: James and Barry Casebere in front of the Unisphere. Photograph courtesy of James Casebere.

Those members of an older generation who attended the earlier 1939/40 Fair as children or young adults, and then returned to the 1964/65 Fair, usually voice disappointment at the later event, often agreeing with its critics. Yet the 1939/40 Fair was in some ways no less a commercial enterprise, although this ulterior motive may have been better disguised then. In *Dawn of a New Day: The New York World's Fair 1939/40*, Helen A. Harrison states:

Conceived as a demonstration of the triumph of enlightened social, economic, and technological engineering, it was actually a monument to merchandising, albeit in a rather more socially responsible guise than was to be seen again for many a decade. The Fair's ostensible message—that foresight and benevolent social guidance would result in a peaceful and prosperous future—was superseded by the more immediate marketing aims of American industry.[3]

So what is recalled from the 1964/65 Fair? Do we agree with its President, Robert Moses, when he said, "The stars of my show are Michelangelo and Walt Disney"?[4] This pairing of the *Pietà* with "It's A Small World"—a mixture of high art with popular culture—created a pop sensibility that pervaded much of the Fair's atmosphere. The noted art critic and historian Katherine Kuh observed:

No one interested in Pop Art should hiss at the hot dog stands proliferating at the Fair, each topped by what resembles huge scoops of glistening white whipped cream. It would take a pretty dynamic pop cartoon, even if monumentally blown up, to divert us from such pleasures, or from the eighty-foot tire that the U.S. Rubber Company has turned into a Ferris wheel.[5]

And critic Vincent J. Scully, Jr. also recognized the pop aspects of the fair:

Chrysler's exhibit, designed by George Nelson, is the surprise of the Fair. It is pop art at its best, and presents Detroit with welcome wit and irony. There is a 'working' engine you can walk into and a demented mock-up of a car of the future you examine from below—the bucket seats are buckets. There is also a zoo of rickety and noisy animals made out of auto parts, some of them looking like the Port Authority helicopters clattering about next door.[6]

The exploitation of the pop style—combining high and low art—to sell a product or a vision was a brilliant move that was readily embraced by both artists and corporations and one that has

Below: Brass Rail restaurants, designed by Victor A. Lundy, Vollmer Associates, and Claude Sampton. Photograph by Bob Golby, collection of The Queens Museum.

Opposite: Aerial view of the Fair showing the U.S. Rubber Ferris Wheel designed by Shreve, Lamb & Harmon Associates. In the background is the Chrysler pavilion. Photograph by Bob Golby, collection of The Queens Museum.

proliferated to this day.

Nowhere was this exploitation more in evidence at the Fair than at the *Pietà* installation in the Vatican pavilion. Katherine Kuh describes it: "All the cumulative pop novelties in the world became urbane by comparison. Accompanied by twinkling electric candles, moving sidewalks, a plastic screen, canned music, chicly costumed usherettes, and an overdose of cold light, the Michelangelo is lost to us forever."[7] Created by Jo Mielziner, the Broadway set designer of such famed productions as *Pal Joey, Annie Get Your Gun,* and *Streetcar Named Desire,* the *Pietà* treatment, with its dramatic lighting, heavy drapery, and mood music, paved the way for blockbuster museum design. Today it is not uncommon for museums

Right: Chrysler pavilion designed by George P. Nelson. One of the largest pavilions of the Fair, this giant car, 20 feet high and 80 feet long, housed an exhibit on automobile styling. Photograph courtesy of Peter M. Warner.

Below, left: Another section of the Chrysler pavilion was an enormous assembly line. Photograph courtesy of Peter M. Warner.

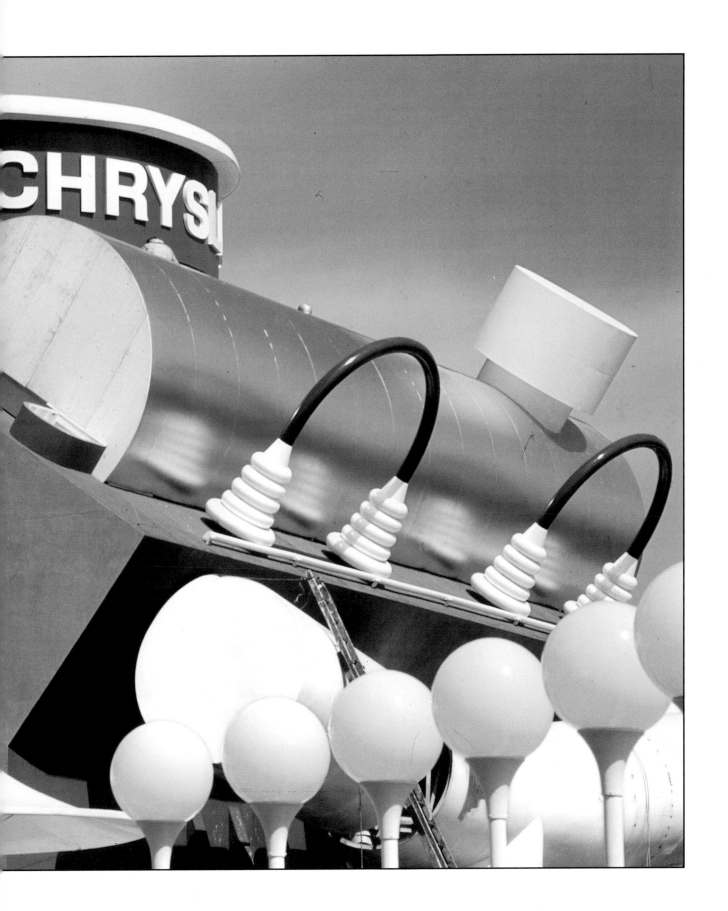

to sell art to their audiences by employing many of the same techniques: objects taken out of context, awash in lurid colors and fabrics, and bathed in department-store lighting. The moving sidewalk—a blatantly anti-aesthetic device—is one of the few aspects of the *Pietà* installation that is not in evidence today.

The Disney presence at the Fair was enormous and its subsequent influence profound. His designed attractions—General Electric's "Carousel of Progress," Pepsi-Cola's "It's a Small World," Ford's "Magic Skyway," and the State of Illinois' "Great Moments with Mr. Lincoln—were tremendously popular, and visitors queued up for hours to see Disney's "Audio-Animatronics" system perfected. Now a staple of theme park wizardry, "Audio-Animatronics" was then in its infancy and had its coming-out party at the Fair.

"Audio-Animatronics," based on an electro-mechanical system, combine and synchronize mechanical movement and sound effects. What one sees is a totally coordinated figure that can sing, dance, and talk. The Disney attractions were not only popular for their sophisticated display techniques, but also for their alluring aspect of providing visitors with a ride. At Ford and Pepsi, visitors were transported through the pavilions in vehicles, and at General Electric the audience moved as the theater rotated between each scene. Not only did the ride aspect of these pavilions contribute to their popularity, but their educational and merchandising aspects were generally disguised within an amusement park sensibility. The other most popular attraction at the Fair, the General Motors "Futurama," was also a ride, although not a Disney production. Pepsi-Cola's "It's a Small World," created in conjunction with UNICEF, was an "Audio-Animatronics" system of hundreds of figures of children, dolls, and toys representing nations throughout the world. Visitors were transported through

Below: Tower of Four Winds sculpture at the entrance to the Pepsi-Cola pavilion. Photograph courtesy of Photofest. © 1989 Walt Disney Company

Opposite: Rolly Crump, designer of the Tower of Four Winds (left) and Walt Disney. Photograph courtesy of The Walt Disney Company. © 1989 Walt Disney Company.

Below: Scenes from "It's a Small World" at the Pepsi-Cola pavilion. This was one of four exhibits designed by Walt Disney Imagineering and featured hundreds of dolls representing children from nations throughout the world.

Top right: Photograph courtesy of Walt Disney Company. © 1989 Walt Disney Company.
Top left: Photograph by Bob Golby, collection of The Queens Museum. © 1989 Walt Disney Company.

Bottom, left: Photograph courtesy of Photofest. © 1989 Walt Disney Company.

Bottom right: Dolls from "It's a Small World." Photograph courtesy of the Rare Books and Manuscripts Division, New York Public Library, Astor, Lenox, and Tilden Foundations. © 1989 Walt Disney Company.

this mechanized world by boat.

For Ford's "Magic Skyway," a twelve-minute "Audio-Animatronics" journey from prehistory to the space age, visitors climbed into one of 160 Ford convertibles, many of them Mustangs, the car that made its debut at the Fair. The ride was programmed in four languages, with narration and music played through the car radio; it began with a journey to a prehistoric jungle and moved through scenes of dinosaur fights to the dawn of mankind and finally to a space city. This display heralded Disney's use of its WEDway Peoplemover system, and it is estimated that fifteen million people rode in the cars, equivalent to sixty-eight trips around the world. This Peoplemoving system made its Disneyland debut in 1967 and is now a staple of theme parks and airports.[8]

The General Electric "Carousel of Progress" presented an "Audio-Animatronics" family that moved through history on a revolving theater to the theme song "It's a Great Big Beautiful Tomorrow." The first scene takes place in 1880, where the family members— mother, father, son, daughter, grandma, grandpa, dog, parrot, and "good ol' Cousin Orville"—pump their water from a well and have no electricity. With a turn of the theater, the family is now in 1920 and electricity is ever present. Television makes its debut in the next scene, and the finale takes place in the present— 1964—where the entire home is programmed to eliminate household chores and the color television presides. The grandparents are no longer in evidence, and the narrator tells us, "You're probably wondering what happened to Grandma and Grandpa. Well, they are no longer with us . . . they have their own home in a community for senior citizens."[9] The State of Illinois' "Great Moments with Mr. Lincoln" was probably the most dramatic use of Audio-Animatronics at the Fair. The three-

Below, top: The Illinois pavilion featured Walt Disney's "Great Moments with Mr. Lincoln." A lifelike figure of Abraham Lincoln addressed the audience with synchronized speech and movements. Photograph courtesy of Walt Disney Company. © 1989 Walt Disney Company.

Below, bottom: Another Walt Disney production was the Ford pavilion's "Magic Skyway." Visitors boarded convertible cars for a twelve-minute "Audio-Animatronics" journey that took them from a prehistoric jungle to a space city. Photograph by Ford Motor Company

News Bureau. Courtesy of Peter M. Warner. © 1989 Walt Disney Company.

Below, top and bottom: At General Electric's "Carousel of Progress," the audience revolved around the stage where an "Audio-Animatronics" family presented the history of electricity. Photographs courtesy of Photofest. © 1989 Walt Disney Company.

dimensional recreation of Lincoln, with synchronized movements and speech reciting excerpts from the Gettysburg Address, was an eerily convincing display.

At the close of the Fair, Walt Disney hoped to establish a theme park on its former site, but Robert Moses flatly refused, insisting that Flushing Meadow become a public park, one to rival Central Park.[10] So Disney decided to move south, and in 1971 Walt Disney World opened in Orlando, Florida. Much of the technology invented and perfected at the 1964 Fair was used at Walt Disney World, and many of the Fair exhibits were relocated there or to Disneyland in Anaheim, California. The original "It's a Small World" went to Disneyland in 1966; in 1965, "Talking Lincoln" was cloned and installed in the Opera House on Main Street at Disneyland, while continuing his performance at the Fair; and the "Carousel of Progress" was moved first to Disneyland, where it played for six years, and then to Walt Disney World, where it is permanently installed, but with one slight difference: Grandma and Grandpa have been reinstated into the family unit in the final scene, having given up their golden-age condominium to settle down with the family.

With the development of EPCOT Center in 1982, the Fair continued to influence theme park technology and philosophy. Today EPCOT is the most tangible evidence of the Fair's legacy, for it aspires to be a permanent world's fair. As described in a 1984 brochure of WED Enterprises, the theme park design arm of the Walt Disney Company, the Fair's impact is clear: "The 'Carousel of Progress' enabled us to expand beyond the realm of fantasy: to educate while we entertain, and it paved the first stretch of the road to EPCOT Center."[11] EPCOT (Experimental Prototype Community of Tomorrow) employs precisely the same combination of elements that provide world's fairs with their unique flavor.

Below: One of the best remembered inventions of the Fair was the "Bel-Gem" waffle. Photograph by James P. Blair. © 1965 National Geographic Society.

Corporate and international government participation is enlisted to create exhibits of technological innovation and international exoticism. EPCOT's two main sections are World Showcase and Futureworld, featuring such exhibits as Bell Systems' "Spaceship Earth," Exxon's "Universe of Energy"; General Motors's "World of Motion," and Kodak's "Journey into the Imagination," and including representation by Japan, China, France, England, Italy, Germany, Canada, and Mexico. Robert Moses would have approved.

Another aspect of the 1964/65 Fair that fostered poignant memories and has provided some resonance to the present was the international flavor that permeated its architecture, food, and entertainment. The largest and most ambitious international environmental creation was the Belgian Village, famous today for having featured one of the best remembered inventions of the Fair—synonymous with its very existence—the "Bel-Gem" Waffle. The exhibition, a meticulous copy of a walled nineteenth-century Flemish village, contained over a hundred houses, a copy of a fifteenth-century church, a city hall, a rathskellar, a canal, and a stone bridge. Attractions in the village, as the Fair's guidebook notes, were "folk dancing, an 1898 carousel, native cuisine, handicrafts and crooked streets lined with small shops. . . ."[12] The village occupied four acres of the Fair, and aside from the waffle, is also remembered for its 1500-seat beer hall, although its other attractions included major masterpieces copied in sand painting, an art form in which the Flemish apparently specialize, and Gille dancers. As the guidebook described them, "Four times each day gaudily dressed clowns wearing wooden shoes, ostrich feather headdresses and bells dance through the streets, accompanied by drums and brass instruments. The Gilles hark back to 1540, when Belgium was ruled by Spain, and the conquistadors' triumph over Peruvian Indians was celebrated at Mardi Gras."[13]

It was the invention of the "Bel-Gem" Waffle that persisted to survive in memory over many other aspects of the Fair. To this day, most people, asked what they remember about the Fair, immediately blurt out "Bel-Gem Waffles," and only then continue to recall other experiences. This food sensation was constructed of a fat, fluffy waffle base that was piled high with a mixture of whipped cream and strawberries; it was available not only in the Belgian Village, but virtually all over the fairgrounds. A fantastic concoction somewhere between a breakfast food and a dessert, the waffle was exotic and sophisticated enough to catch the public's attention. Although the "Bel-Gem" Waffle fad did not last, the name still appears on the menus of the International House of Pancakes and on those of certain diners across the country.

The Fair boasted many other types of cuisines in its more than 112 restaurants, and for many, their samplings of these became memorable moments. It should be remembered that in 1964, international dining and "continental cuisine" were not nearly as commonplace as they are in America today. At the Hawaii pavilion, in the Five Volcanos Restaurant and Lava Pit Bar, one could participate in a luau; at the India pavilion one could experience tandoori and paratha; the Republic of Korea offered kimchi; the Japan pavilion featured two restaurants, and one could taste sukiyaki and tempura; at Lebanon one could try markouk; at Jordan homas and shaurmah were available; and at the Tree House Restaurant in the African pavilion, the adventurous could sample ". . . special delicacies of a number of regions including chicken, lamb and pork dishes garnished with a peanut sauce."[14]

While Walt Disney was promoting

Below: The Belgian Village, designed by Alfons de Rijdt and Hooks & Wax occupied four acres at the Fair. Photograph courtesy of the Rare Books and Manuscripts Division, New York Public Library, Astor, Lenox, and Tilden Foundations.

world unification and equality among men, Wycliffe Bible Translators, sponsor of the "2,000 Tribes Pavilion," was suggesting that white supremacy conquer Latin America. Its souvenir brochure, entitled *From Savage to Citizen,* depicts the world of "savage tribes" and their transformation into civilized beings through the discovery of Jesus and the Bible, brought to them by missionary white girls. The brochure copy begins:

I was an unhappy savage chief. I used to cut off the heads at the shoulders, then cut the back of the head for scalping. I loved to kill— I took many heads. We went on raids. We speared, we killed, we hated . . . We set fire to the houses. . . ." Chief Tariri learned from his forefathers to hate, and kill, and shrink the heads of his enemies. He plundered and murdered in an isolated corner of the great Amazon River basin.

The story proceeds to relate the coming of the missionaries, who told the savages to "Take Jesus" and become civilized. "We fervently loved Satan—the boa is really Satan," says Tariri. "Now that we love Jesus and have taken Him as the missionaries have taught us, we have done away with boa worship. We want no more of that."[20]

The 1939 Fair also left much debris in the way of souvenir brochures, and some of the most provocative and alluring were those from the amusement zone. Morris Gest's Midget Town booklet not only contains photographs and programs for the performances, but articles with such headings as "Midget-Dwarf-Pigmy-Lilliputian What is the Difference?"; "Midget Weddings," and "Can Midgets Have Babies?" The brochure for *Michael Todd's Hall of Music Presents Streets of Paris* depicts a scantily clad Gypsy Rose Lee on the cover. Inside, the program is profusely illustrated with half-naked women and there is an article on Miss Lee entitled "She Strips to Conquer."

The more material legacy of the 1964/65 Fair is composed of its souvenirs. How the Fair was merchandised can best be understood both in the context of the age and in comparison to the presentation of the 1939/40 Fair, for both bear witness to the commercial nature of each event.

In *Dawn of A New Day: The New York World's Fair 1939/40,* Warren Susman noted:

This Fair, more than had any previous effort, promoted as a major purpose the availability of consumer goods and services. It was a Fair that from the very start viewed the people not only as observers but as potential customers of the products it displayed. Thus, the advertising potential of the Fair and its promotion of the growing consumer culture of the time marked a subtle change in the role of the Fair—for the people.[15]

Manufacturers seized the opportunity to exploit the 1939/40 Fair and its utopian vision of the future to advertise and sell their products. By emblazoning the Trylon and Perisphere—the theme center symbol—on their wares, merchandisers could associate their goods with the Fair, and thus the consumer could buy into the dream that the Fair was selling. In 1939, there was no television, and hence no commercials; advertising was limited to print and radio, where the consumer could neither get the full visual effect of a product or see how it performed. The Fair represented a potentially large consumer pool—22 million visited the event—and many companies wanted to jump on its bandwagon. The Fair Corporation minutes of February 14, 1939 list a wide range of companies that applied for and received licensing permission for their products. The Germain Seed and Plant Co. was given the privilege of selling and promoting a New York World's Fair Sweet Pea; C.A. Grosvenor Shoe Co. was able to sell and manufacture "The Trylon Sandal, a sandal made with either leather or rubber sole, the upper being a braided or woven stripping containing a design resembling the Trylon and Perisphere. . . ."[16] The Hygiene Shower Curtain Manufacturing Co. could sell shower and window curtains that matched; Leona Undergarment Co. officially manufactured ladies' slips, and

Below: John Atherton, *1939 World's Fair Poster.* Collection of The Queens Museum, purchased with funds from the George and Mollie Wolfe World's Fair Fund. Photograph by Jim Strong. Courtesy of The Queens Museum.

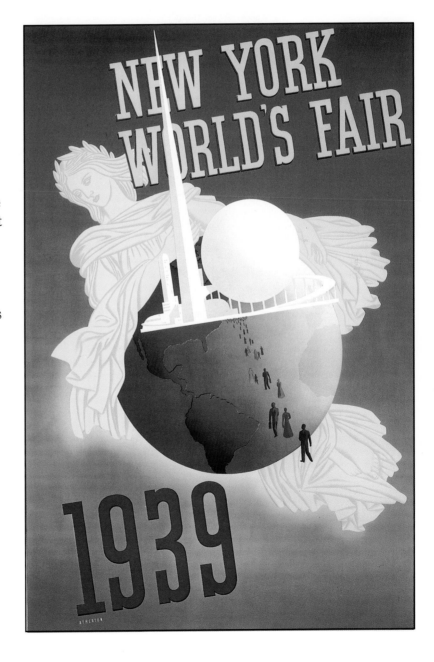

Below, top right and left: Souvenirs from the 1939/40 World's Fair: enamel-top table, wooden chair with Trylon and Perisphere, George Washington dinner plate, Trylon and Perisphere salt and pepper shakers, drinking glass, and silverware; Trylon and Perisphere pitcher made by

Porceliers; Tiffany and Company commemorative plate. Collection of The Queens Museum, purchased with funds from The George and Mollie Wolfe World's Fair Fund. Photographs by Jim Strong, courtesy of The Queens Museum.

Below, bottom: R.C.A. Victor radio with Trylon and Perisphere design, 1939. Collection of The Queens Museum, purchase. Photograph by Phyllis Bilick, courtesy of The Queens Museum.

Allen B. Wrisley sold Trylon and Perisphere bath soap. And so the 1939/40 Fair invaded every corner of the consumer's life, including their bathrooms and underwear!

Ordinary household products that did not fit into the traditional souvenir genre were also plastered with the Trylon and Perisphere and marketed on the Fair's coattails. Items included the Bissell Carpet Sweeper, radios by R.C.A. Victor and Crosley, General Electric clocks, Kodak Bullet and Baby Brownie cameras, Remington's Close Shaver Razor and Cadet Typewriter, and Knapp-Monarch's electric fan—all bore World's Fair identification to cash in on the consumer consciousness. More conventional souvenir fare also was produced, items made of inexpensive materials that functioned to commemorate the event, thinly disguised in a cloak of functionalism. Ladies' compacts, cigarette lighters, ashtrays, plates, postcards, salt and pepper shakers, savings banks, and pocket knives, among other items, were all marketed for the event.

It is illuminating to compare the 1939 board game, "Going to the World's Fair," with its 1964 counterpart, "The World's Fair Game." In the 1939 version, the directions state the following objective:

The design of the playing board depicts the "theme center" of the fair, represented by the "trylon," a slender obelisk rising 700 feet into the air, and the "perisphere," a pure white ball 200 feet in diameter, together with some of the prominent exhibit buildings and the amusement zone which the players are supposed to visit. Within the "perisphere" is a magic carpet, a chart from which is determined the amount of money a player must pay for the amusement visited and the amount he wins or loses while engaged in the games of skill or chance. The object of the game is to see which of the players has the most money after he has made a complete tour of the fair.

The 1964 game makes no mention of money, and its goals are slightly loftier, in keeping with Robert Moses's idea of the Fair. The object here is to absorb as much "knowledge" as possible by visiting the greatest number of exhibits:

The theme of the World's Fair is "Peace through Understanding." This is symbolized by the "Unisphere," which is located near the center of the Fair. Surrounding it are different areas. Everyone interested in the "FAIR" will enjoy playing this game, as each turn is like a "Day at the Fair." Using Exhibit cards, the players visit as many ADJOINING Areas in a "day" (turn) as they can, to score points.

The marketing of souvenirs for the 1964/65 Fair demonstrated how merchandising and consumer attitudes had changed since 1939. With television's stronghold on the mainstream of society, manufacturers no longer needed to associate their products with the Fair to stimulate sales. Television advertising was a powerful force that manipulated the consumer culture with much greater muscle than the Fair could ever do. People had more time and money to spend on leisure, and on purchasing non-functional items. In his book *Populuxe*, Thomas Hines discusses this trend as it applied to the late fifties:

An unprecedented distribution of disposable income had created a disposable world. Use it once and throw it away was the promise of many consumer products. The concept of planned obsolescence, pioneered by General Motors during the 1920s, was commonly understood, and accepted. Artifacts were specifically designed not to last. The object was not the object. Rather the goal was production, sales and continued economic activity.[17]

This dynamic translated to the souvenir market of the Fair meant that items did not need to masquerade as functional or useful (although some did retain this added allure); rather, they could merely commemorate the event.

Mass-produced objects made of cheap materials were meant to last as long as the memory of the event could be sustained. Some of the official souvenirs of the Fair marketed by its licensing division included: oil paintings, paperweights, calendars, greeting cards, gift wraps, postcards, knife novelties, glassware, stamped metal ashtrays, canisters, pendants, official medallions, playing cards, and outdoor and indoor flags. Made out of paper, inexpensive china, metal and plastic, all bore the

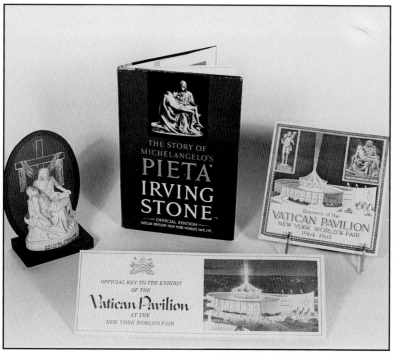

ubiquitous logo of the Unisphere. There was also an array of products shaped like the space-age globe, mostly in the color silver, which seemed to have had a certain cache in the 1960s. Andy Warhol noted: "Silver was the future, it was spacey—the astronauts wore silver suits—Shepard, Grissom, and Glenn had already been up in them, and their equipment was silver, too. And silver was also the past—the Silver Screen—Hollywood actresses photographed in silver sets."[18]

Aside from the officially licensed Fair souvenirs, every individual pavilion produced for sale or as a give-away pamphlets, buttons, models, records, and innumerable other items promoting its particular display. One of the most commercial of these enterprises, the Vatican pavilion, offered a vast array of items. Among them was a *Pietà* replica on a blue base, mimicking the installation; recordings of the pavilion background music and of the highlights of Pope Paul VI's trip to America; the *Story of Michelangelo's Pietà,* a hardbound book by Irving Stone; an official souvenir ceramic tile meant to hang on a wall; the *Official Guide to the Vatican Pavilion;* and a button depicting the Pope with hands clasped and inscribed "Pray for Peace, Pope Paul VI." The marketing opportunities seemed endless, and popular items from other pavilions that survived with great tenacity include molded plastic dinosaurs from Sinclair Dinoland and a miniature toy Uniroyal Tire Ferris Wheel. Most pavilions, though, simply produced commemorative souvenir brochures. One of the most elaborate of these was *Walt Disney's It's a Small World.* This "complete souvenir guide and behind the scenes story" depicts in full color the installation's ride sequence and grand finale scene, and contains a souvenir map, photos, and text describing the creation of the pavilion, along with the lyrics to the "Small World"

Below: Whitney Darrow, Jr., *1964 New York World's Fair Poster*. Collection of The Queens Museum, purchase. Photograph by Phyllis Bilick, courtesy of The Queens Museum.

Left and below: Many pavilions created their own souvenirs for marketing purposes. These included a miniature Ferris Wheel toy from U.S. Rubber and molded plastic dinosaur replicas from Sinclair Dinoland. Collection of The Queens Museum, purchase. Photographs by Phyllis Bilick, courtesy of The Queens Museum.

DON'T MEET ME IN ST. LOUIS, LOUIE,

...MEET ME AT THE FAIR

---POGO

theme song, which to this day can still be recalled by millions of fairgoers. But just in case, the words to the first verse are:

It's a world of laughter, a world of tears
It's a world of hopes and a world of fears
There's so much that we share
That it's time we're aware
It's a Small World after all.[19]

Fortunately, a tangible legacy was left not only by 1964/65 pavilion sponsors and the Fair Corporation, but also by prominent cartoonists, artists, and photographers who chose to immortalize and poke fun at the Fair. Al Capp and Walt Kelly, popular cartoonists of the day, promoted the 1964/65 Fair in their comic strips, and Milton Caniff, the creator of Steve Canyon, designed a special Fair brochure that was distributed to all Fair employees. Entitled *Poteet Canyon Press Aide at the New York World's Fair,* it relates the tale of Steve Canyon's niece, fresh from a midwestern university, arriving at the Fair for summer employment and a coming-of-age adventure. Archie, Jughead, Veronica, Betty, and Reggie all visited the Fair in a special issue, *Life with Archie,* (November 1964), and in the first couple of pages the symbol of the Unisphere abounds, as do double entendre jokes as the Archie gang schemes its way to the Fair. *The Flintstones at The New York World's Fair* commemorates the visit of the "modern stone age family" and relates their adventures, including that of Dino, the family pet dinosaur, who has the misfortune of falling in love with a life-size papier-mache dinosaur replica at Sinclair's Dinoland. The cartoonists Ronald Searles, whose illustrations appeared in *Holiday,* and Rube Goldberg, the creator of wacky, fantastically cumbersome machines that perform simple tasks, tackled the timely topic of World's Fair feet, a syndrome that afflicted many fairgoers in 1964. The Fair also provided fodder for *New Yorker* cartoonists Charles Addams, Peter Arno, Ed Fields, George Price, and Carl Rose,

Below, top: Lil Abner cartoon by Al Capp. Photograph courtesy of the Rare Books and Manuscripts Division, New York Public Library, Astor, Lenox, and Tilden Foundations. © 1961 Capp Enterprises, Inc. All rights reserved.

Below, bottom: Official Souvenir, *The Flintstones at the New York World's Fair* comic book. Collection of The Queens Museum, purchase. Photograph courtesy of The Queens Museum.

Below: Ronald Searles, *Tired Feet Wading in the Unisphere Pool.* One of a series of illustrations that Searles did for the July 1964 issue of *Holiday.* Photograph courtesy of John Locke Studios, Inc.

among others, who chided many aspects of both the 1939/40 and 1964/65 Fairs, commenting on everything from Robert Moses and Grover Whalen to the House of Good Taste and the Electrified Farm.

Straddling popular and fine art, Roy Lichtenstein created a special World's Fair cover for the April 1964 issue of *Art in America.* In a marvelous pop interpretation of the Fair, Lichtenstein uses comic superhero language against a Fair backdrop. Many of the diverse architectural styles that the Fair contained are jammed into the image, while a gas-masked figure in the forefront comments on technological society. Although the Fair is not the main focus of James Rosenquist's painting, *"That margin between that which men naturally do and that which they can is so great that a system which urges men to action and develops individual enterprise and initiative is preferable in spite of the wastes that necessarily attend that process." Louis Dembitz Brandeis 1856–1941,* he incorporated the symbol of the Unisphere as one of several elements—along with a car door and strands of spaghetti—as an icon of consumer culture. A younger

generation of artists has continued to embody the symbols of the two Fairs—the Trylon and Perisphere and the Unisphere—to comment on our current consumer and technological society. Such works as Richard Haas's *Japanese Realtors' Tower, Flushing Meadows, N.Y.,* John Bowman's *Another World,* and Claudia DeMonte's *Commemorative Column* clearly demonstrate that the fairs' logos continue to evoke a strong symbolic presence.

For photographers, the fairs provided endless opportunities to capture society, technology, and architecture in a condensed atmosphere, and for some they provided a chance to explore abstraction. Yasuo Kuniyoshi's *World's Fair Ceiling,* 1939, looks down on a glass-enclosed structure, depicting a strong interplay of shadows and fractured images. The ever-present Weegee attached an inexpensive kaleidoscope to his camera lens to take a series of pictures from 1964 of multiple images of easily recognizable Fair icons. Other memorable photographs of the 1964/65 Fair include those by Cornell Capa, whose series of images of the IBM pavilion

Opposite: Weegee (Arthur Felig) attached a kaleidoscope to his camera to take photographs of the Fair. Shown is the Florida pavilion. Photograph courtesy of UPI/Bettmann Newsphotos.

Below: Garry Winogrand, *World's Fair, New York City,* 1964. Photograph courtesy of Fraenkel Gallery San Francisco and The Estate of Garry Winogrand.

Right: Cornell Capa, *Cleaning the Roof,* IBM pavilion, 1964. Photograph courtesy of Cornell Capa/ Magnum Photos Inc.

exterior and interior exhibits are evocative juxtapositions of man in a technological society; Garry Winogrand's image of women seated on a bench at the Fair; and Bruce Davidson's series of photographs that use the Fair as a metaphor for environmental destruction.

How world's fairs have become woven into our national consciousness is poignantly evoked by E. L. Doctorow's depiction of the 1939/40 Fair in his novel, *World's Fair*. The protagonist, nine-year-old Edgar, visits the Fair twice, once with a friend and her mother, who works in the Amusement Zone wrestling Oscar the Amorous Octopus, and once with his family. Upon seeing the Trylon and Perisphere, Edgar exclaims:

They were white in the sun, white spire, white globe, they went together, they belonged together as some sort of partnership in my head. I didn't know what they stood for, it was all very vague in my mind, but to see them, after having seen pictures and posters and buttons of them for so long, made me incredibly happy.[21]

Surely a younger generation of writers will be inspired by their own memories of the 1964/65 Fair.

Both Fairs' symbols continue to provide powerful memories: people met at them, got married there, had their first glimpse of technological wonders, and savored hundreds of other such experiences. Yet in the late twentieth century, the Fairs' significance as cultural and technological barometers has certainly dwindled, and it is easy to regard them with cynicism. With the advancement of communications and the rapid rate at which we receive visual and factual information, a world's fair can hardly document the present, let alone predict the future. As Walt Disney insisted, "It's a Small World," and the impact of that message is still being felt, making world's fairs, an outmoded concept, their place usurped by the very theme parks they spawned. Nevertheless, the 1964/65 World's Fair maintains a strong hold on the collective imagination and will continue to do so for years to come.

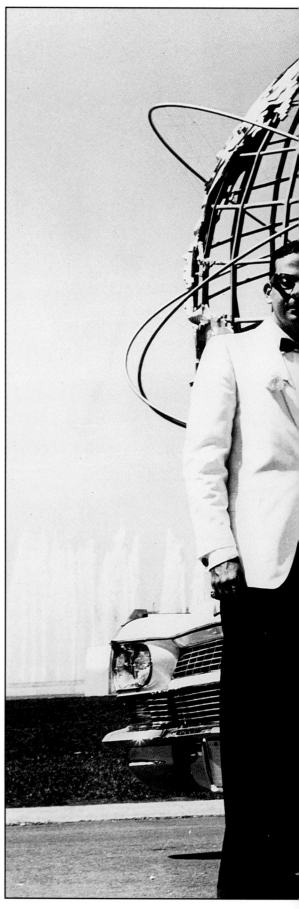

Right: Couple married at the Fair. Photograph courtesy of the Rare Books and Manuscripts Division, New York Public Library, Astor, Lenox, and Tilden Foundations.

Below: Demolition of the
Underground House.
Photograph by Bruce
Davidson, © Bruce
Davidson/Magnum Photos,
Inc.

Below: Demolition of the Hawaii pavilion, 1965. Photograph by Peter M. Warner.

Right: The dismantling of Sinclair Dinoland, 1965. Photograph courtesy of *The New York Daily News*.

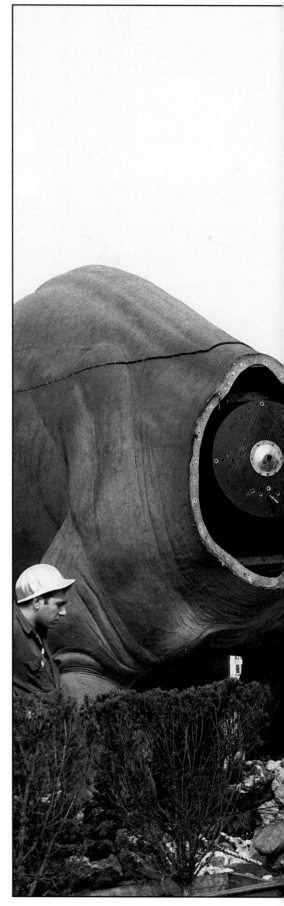

Opposite: Demolition of the IBM pavilion. Photograph courtesy of Photofest.

Below: Demolition of the 1964/65 World's Fair. Photograph by Bruce Davidson, © Bruce Davidson/Magnum Photos, Inc.

N O T E S

Chapter One/Dickstein

1. Kenneth W. Luckhurst, *The Story of Exhibitions* (London & New York: Studio Publications, 1951), p. 163. "Piercing the sky 700 feet above the earth like some giant three-sided obelisk, *the Trylon*, symbol of the Fair's lofty purpose, adjoins a huge hollow globe, 200 feet in diameter—*the Perisphere*," says the guidebook in the hyperbolic style that seems obligatory for describing such scenes. "Never before in history has man undertaken to build a globe of such tremendous proportions. Eighteen stories high, it is as broad as a city block, its interior more than twice the size of the Radio City Music Hall." *Official Guide Book, New York World's Fair 1939* (New York: Exposition Publications, 1939), p. 43.
2. *Official Guide Book*, p. 208.
3. *Official Guide Book*, p. 44.
4. E. L. Doctorow, *World's Fair* (New York: Random House, 1985).
5. E. L. Doctorow, *World's Fair*, pp. 252–253.
6. Godfrey Hodgson, *America in Our Time* (Garden City, N.Y.: Doubleday, 1976), p. 19.
7. "Next to home and family, the American loved his car most. Car buyers were usually male. . . . After the war there was no material thing the American man wanted more than a new car, except, if married, a new house. No civilian vehicles had been produced since 1942 and the existing stock was antiquated." William L. O'Neill, *American High: The Years of Confidence, 1945–60* (New York: The Free Press, 1986), p. 29.
8. William E. Leuchtenburg, *A Troubled Feast: American Society Since 1945* (Boston: Little Brown & Company, 1973), pp. 55, 58.
9. William E. Leuchtenburg, *Franklin D. Roosevelt and the New Deal, 1932–1940* (New York: Harper & Row, 1963), pp. 157–158.
10. Roberta Strauss Feuerlicht, "God and Man At Flushing Meadow," *The Reporter*, August 13, 1964, p. 54.
11. See William L. O'Neill, *American High*, pp. 212–215. Church membership rose from 64.5 million in 1940 to 114.5 million in 1960. But as O'Neill comments, paraphrasing sociologist Will Herberg, American religion was "not so much a matter of worship as a search for meaning and identity. The American Way of Life, not Christianity, was the real religion of the country."
12. Sidney M. Shalett, "Epitaph for The World's Fair," *Harper's*, December 1940, pp. 23–24.
13. Peter Lyon, "A Glorious Nightmare," *Holiday*, July 1964, p. 50. This lively article contains perhaps the best overall description of many features of the 1964 Fair.
14. Robert A. Caro, *The Power Broker: Robert Moses and the Fall of New York* (New York: Alfred A. Knopf, 1974), pp. 1106–1107.
15. According to Martin Mayer, when Moses's name was first mentioned, the man who originated the idea for the Fair, a lawyer named Robert Koppel who had once tangled with Moses, objected that "he was too old, lacked the showman's instinct, and had got his remarkable results as a public official by browbeating people rather than persuading them, a technique that would not bring foreign governments or big corporations to the Fair." Though the big corporations came, the rest of this proved prophetic. When the job was offered to Moses, he accepted "on one condition—that the committee release Koppel." Martin Mayer, "Ho Hum, Come To The Fair," *Esquire*, October 1963, p. 124.
16. Robert A. Caro, *The Power Broker*, p. 1102.
17. On the ethnological (and often racist) elements in early American fairs, see Robert W. Rydell, *All the World's a Fair: Visions of Empire at American International Expositions, 1876–1916* (Chicago: University of Chicago Press, 1984), especially the pages on the Columbian Exposition, pp. 38–71.
18. *Life*, May 1, 1964, p. 28, described this as an electronic city, "a Utopian metropolis that has no slums or parking problems. Traffic moves under electronic control with hardly a dented fender or cross word." A GM press release seemed to envision the city on the model of a modern airport, concerned above all with smooth vehicular flow: "The transportation towers which operate as the city's nerve center monitor all traffic entering, leaving or by-passing the metropolis. Computers inventory destination, speed, best routes and parking as motorists check-in electronically with the transportation control centers." The "Futurama" applied the computer-control model to farming, undersea life, and weather-monitoring in the antarctic. It was the social vision of men who might have played with model trains.
19. Peter Lyon, "A Glorious Nightmare," *Holiday*, July 1964, p. 54.
20. Quoted by Joseph P. Cusker, "The World of Tomorrow: Science, Culture, and Community at the New York World's Fair," in Helen A. Harrison, ed., *Dawn of a New Day: The New York World's Fair, 1939/40* (New York: The Queens Museum and New York University Press, 1980), p. 4.
21. David Nevin, "The Show Goes On, the Spoilers Lose the Day," *Life*, May 1, 1964, p. 35.
22. Robert A. Caro, *The Power Broker*, p. 1101.
23. Richard Schickel, *The Disney Version: The Life, Times, Art and Commerce of Walt Disney* (New York: Simon and Schuster, 1968), p. 335.
24. "It's A Small World," Dioramas from Ford's "Magic Skyway," and The GE "Carousel of Progress" also were transported to Disneyland, and eventually to Walt Disney World near Orlando, Florida. Epcot Center, Disney's other Florida operation, created, in a sense, a permanent world's fair atmosphere.
25. Garry Wills, *Reagan's America: Innocents at Home* (London: Heinemann, 1988), p. 387.
26. Stanley Appelbaum, ed., *The New York World's Fair 1939/40* (New York: Dover, 1977), p. xii. This book, composed mainly of photographs by Richard Wurts, is an invaluable help in any effort to reconstruct the physical aspect of the 1939 Fair. One of the best verbal descriptions of the Fair is by Alice G. Marquis in *Hopes and Ashes: The Birth of Modern Times, 1929–1939* (New York: The Free Press, 1986), pp. 187–231. The best overall interpretation of the Fair in the context of thirties culture remains Warren I. Susman's "The People's Fair: Cultural Contradictions of a Consumer Society," in Helen A. Harrison, ed., *Dawn of a New Day*, pp. 17–27. Also see Susman's book *Culture As History: The Transformation of American Society in the Twentieth Century* (New York: Pantheon, 1985), pp. 211–229.
27. Eric Salzman, "Come to the Fair Anyway," *New York Herald Tribune Sunday Magazine*, July 19, 1964, p. 5.

Chapter Two/Miller

1. Anonymous, "Robert (Or-I'll-Resign) Moses," *Fortune*, June 1938, p. 138; Robert A. Caro, *The Power Broker: Robert Moses and the Fall of New York* (New York: Alfred A. Knopf, 1974); Laura Rosen, "Robert Moses And New York: The Early Years," *The Livable City* (New York: The Municipal Art Society, December 1988).

2. Robert Moses, "From Dump to Glory," *Saturday Evening Post*, January 15, 1938.

3. *The Flushing Meadow Improvement: Final Publication with Complete Résumé of all Improvements to Date Together with Plan and Sketches For the Construction of Flushing Meadow Park After The Fair*, Official Publication of the City and State Officials in Charge of Basic Improvements at Flushing Meadow Park, 1938; Eugene A. Santomasso, "The Design of Reason: Architecture and Planning at the 1939/40 New York World's Fair," in Helen A. Harrison, ed., *Dawn of a New Day: The New York World's Fair, 1939/40* (New York: The Queens Museum and New York University Press, 1980), pp. 31–32.

4. "Glass Diorama to House City's Exhibit," *The Flushing Meadow Improvement*, December 1936, pp. 9–12; "Plan of New York State World's Fair Commission For A Water Amphitheatre On The Meadow, *The Flushing Meadow Improvement*, November 1936, p. 12.

5. "Street Improvements Planned For Fair," *The Flushing Meadow Improvement*, December 1936, pp. 6–7.

6. "Flushing Meadow Park To Become Versailles of America After Fair," *The Flushing Meadow Improvement*, October 1936, pp. 1–2.

7. Robert Caro, *The Power Broker*, pp. 1059–1081.

8. The development of the 1964/65 World's Fair and related projects is charted in the ten issues of the New York World's Fair 1964–1965 Corporation progress reports, *New York World's Fair 1964–1965*, 1961–1965.

9. Robert Moses, *Public Works: A Dangerous Trade* (New York: McGraw-Hill, 1970), p. 549.

10. *Implications Of The New York World's Fair: Remarks of Robert Moses to Students at Brandeis University, Waltham, Massachusetts, Thursday Evening, March 23, 1961*, no publisher, no date, pp. 8–9.

11. *New York World's Fair 1964–1965*, Issue One, January 16, 1961, p. 2.

12. Memorandum, Moses to Constable, July 21, 1960. Theme Committee folder, Container 58, New York World's Fair 1964–1965 Corporation Records, The New York Public Library Rare Books And Manuscripts Division (hereafter cited as NYPL).

13. Letter, Teague to Moses, May 19, 1960; letter, Teague to John S. Young, December 2, 1960. Theme Committee folder, Container 58, NYPL.

14. Letter, Moses to Clarke, August 12, 1960. Theme Committee folder, Container 58, NYPL.

15. "Presentation Book of Portland Cement Association Exhibit at World's Fair," Working Drawings & Models folder, Container 142, New York World's Fair 1964–1965 Corporation Records, NYPL; Anonymous, "Moon-Viewing Platform Shows Concrete," *Progressive Architecture News Report*, July 1961, p. 45.

16. William Robbins, "Doodle Grew Into The Unisphere, With Help From a Rubber Ball," *New York Times*, August 16, 1964; *How to Make a Unisphere*, Remarks by Austin J. Paddock, Administrative Vice President, Fabrication and Manufacture, United States Steel Corporation, Before the Board of Directors, New York World's Fair, March 13, 1962. Construction-Theme folder, Container 109, New York World's Fair 1964–1965 Corporation Records, NYPL.

17. New York World's Fair 1964–1965 Corporation, *Post Fair Expansion Hall of Science*, pamphlet, February 24, 1964.

18. John Molleson, "Model City," *New York Herald Tribune Sunday Magazine*, July 12, 1964, pp. 5–7.

19. Robert Moses, "From Dump to Glory."

20. Vincent J. Scully, Jr., "If This Is Architecture, God Help Us," *Life*, July 31, 1964.

21. Robert Moses, *The Fair, The City, and The Critics*, pamphlet, New York World's Fair 1964–65 Corporation, October 13, 1964, p. 7.

22. Robert Moses, *The Fair, The City, and the Critics*, p. 2.

23. Interview with Harold Blake, October 22, 1988.

24. Robert Caro, *The Power Broker*, pp. 1112–1113.

Chapter Three/Reaven

1. *Newsday*, September 4, 1988.

2. William J. Miller, "It Began with Xerxes," in Norman P. Ross, ed., *Official Souvenir Book, New York World's Fair 1964/1965* (New York: Time-Life Books, 1964), p. 93.

3. Peter Lyon, "A Glorious Nightmare," *Holiday*, July 1964, p. 50.

4. Peter Lyon, p. 57.

5. William L. Laurence, *Science at the Fair*, (New York: New York World's Fair 1964–1965 Corporation, 1964), p. 41.

6. William L. Laurence, p. 43 (emphasis added).

7. *The General Electric Monogram* (company newsletter), April 1964, pp. 6–7.

8. The A.E.C. also promised to contribute about $5 million in equipment to a planned post-Fair "nuclear museum" that would have been built (with $3 million from New York City) next to the Hall of Science.

9. From "There's a Great, Big, Beautiful Tomorrow," lyrics and music by Richard M. Sherman and Robert B. Sherman, © 1963 Wonderland Music Co., Inc.

10. Bradd Schiffman, "Du Pont at the 1964/65 New York World's Fair," *Fair News*, vol. 19, no. 5, undated, p. 14.

11. Nuclear physicist Willard Cheek, quoted in Peter Lyon, p. 56.

12. Quoted in *20th Anniversary: A Disney Retrospective*, New York World's Fair 1964–1965 (Walt Disney Productions, 1984) p. 7.

13. See Joseph P. Cusker, "The World of Tomorrow: Science, Culture, and Community at the New York World's Fair," in Helen A. Harrison, ed., *Dawn of a New Day: The New York World's Fair, 1939/40* (New York: The Queens Museum and New York University Press, 1980), pp. 3–15.

14. "Narration for Futurama Ride," 4th revision, General Motors Corporation, 1964–65 New York World's Fair, March 2, 1964, p. 2.

15. An engineering achievement itself; see "A Design Summary of the GM Futurama II Ride at the 1964–65 New York World's Fair," *General Motors Engineering Journal*, vol. II, No. 2, second quarter, 1964, pp. 1–10.

16. "Narration for Futurama Ride," p. 8.

17. Film director Fritz Lang visited New York in 1924 and then made *Metropolis*.

. "Lang's picture made such an impression on the minds of the whole Western world that nobody can think of portraying the future except in terms of towers connected by ramps—when what people are actually thinking about today are wide-open spaces and park-like areas of green." Saul David, quoted in Philip Strick, "The Metropolis Wars: The City as Character in Science Fiction Films," in Danny Peary, ed., *Omni's Screen Flights/Screen Fantasies: The Future According to Science Fiction Cinema* (New York: Doubleday & Co., 1984), p. 46. Lang's film also influenced the classics *Just Imagine* (1930) and *Things to Come*, and all of this no doubt influenced the design of the 1939 "Futurama."

18. Peter Lyon, p. 54.

19. Robert Malone, "Whose Tomorrow?", *Industrial Design*, May 1964, p. 35.

20. See, for example, the debate reported in Craig R. Whitney, "Can a Film Do Justice to Literature?" *New York Times*, February 11, 1989.

21. Norman P. Ross, ed., *Official Souvenir Book*, p. 21.

Chapter Four/Bletter

1. [Douglas Haskell] editorial, "The Arrested Development of the New York Fair," *Architectural Forum*, December 1960, p. 61; editorial, "Fair is (so far) Foul," *Industrial Design*, March 1961, p. 27; Hedy Backlin, "The Laissez-Fair," *Craft Horizons*, September–October 1963, pp. 40–41.

2. Eugene A. Santomasso, "The Design of Reason: Architecture and Planning at the 1939/40 World's Fair," Helen A. Harrison, ed., *Dawn of a New Day: The New York World's Fair, 1939/40* (New York: The Queens Museum and New York University Press, 1980), p. 39.

3. Robert A. Caro, *The Power Broker: Robert Moses and the Fall of New York* (New York: Alfred A. Knopf, 1974), pp. 1092 ff., and Ursula Cliff, "Fair and Square," *Industrial Design*, March 1961, p. 39.

4. Robert A. Caro, p. 1093, and Ursula Cliff, p. 40.

5. Ursula Cliff, p. 41.

6. Robert A. Caro, pp. 1089 and 1101.

7. Ursula Cliff, p. 38.

8. Ursula Cliff, pp. 40–41.

9. Douglas Haskell, p. 61.

10. Peter Lyon, "A Glorious Nightmare," *Holiday*, July 1964, p. 50.

11. [M. M.] "All's Fair . . . ," *Industrial Design*, March 1964, p. 47.

12. Douglas Haskell, p. 61.

13. Peter Lyon, p. 64; Ellen Perry, James T. Burns, and Jan Rowan, "The Busy Architect's Guide to the World's Fair," *Progressive Architecture*, October 1964, p. 229; no author,

"Queen of the Fair," *Progressive Architecture,* December 1964, pp. 160–167; Ada Louise Huxtable, "World's Fair: International Scope," *New York Times,* Sunday, May 10, 1964, Art, p. 19.

14. Ellen Perry et. al., p. 229. See also Ada Louise Huxtable, p. 19.

15. IBM press release, 1961; Kevin Roche, John Dinkeloo & Associates, undated press release; *IBM Fair,* souvenir book, IBM Corporation, unpaged; John E.T. Van Duyl, "The Unforgettable IBM Pavilion at the New York World's Fair of 1964," *World's Fair,* Fall 1987, pp. 9–11; and "Best of the Fair: 4 Distinguished Statements," *Interiors,* October 1964, p. 127.

16. *IBM Fair.*

17. Quoted in John E.T. Van Duyl, p. 11.

18. Ellen Perry et. al., p. 226.

19. Ellen Perry et. al., p. 232.

20. Frank Lloyd Wright, *An Autobiography* (New York: Horizon Press, 1977), pp. 380–381.

21. Larry Zim, Mel Lerner, and Herbert Rolfes, *The World of Tomorrow: The 1939 New York World's Fair* (New York: Harper & Row, 1988), p. 110. See also Helen A. Harrison, ed., *Dawn of a New Day.*

22. Peter Lyon, pp. 53–54.

23. Ellen Perry et. al., p. 235.

24. There is no catalogue for this important Museum of Modern Art exhibition organized by Arthur Drexler. However, excerpts from Drexler's labels are in the Museum's library.

25. Unless otherwise noted, all information about the second version of "Futurama" is from General Motors's press releases about the exhibit.

26. Emilio Ambasz, ed., *Italy: The New Domestic Landscape: Achievements and Problems of Italian Design* (New York: The Museum of Modern Art, 1972).

27. Ellen Perry et. al., p. 235.

28. "Moon-Viewing Platform Shows Concrete," *Progressive Architecture,* July 1961, p. 45, and interview with Paul Rudolph, March 24, 1989.

29. General Electric, undated press release.

30. Ellen Perry et. al., p. 229.

31. General Electric, undated press release, and *The Mighty Fair: New York World's Fair 1964–1965: A Retrospective,* exhibition catalogue (New York: Flushing Gallery, 1985), p. 15.

32. Ellen Perry et. al., p. 233.

33. Jay Swayze, *Underground Gardens and Homes: The Best of Two Worlds—Above and Below* (Hereford, Texas: Geobuilding Systems, 1980), p. 19.

34. Jay Swayze, p. 20.

35. Rosemarie Haag Bletter, "The World of Tomorrow: The Future With a Past," *High Styles: Twentieth-Century American Design* (New York: Whitney Museum of American Art, 1985), pp. 84 ff. Prohibition and the greater need to entertain at home, as well as more informal life styles, also influenced the transformation of the front parlor into the family room.

36. Peter Lyon, p. 62.

37. Peter Lyon, pp. 62–64.

38. "Razzmatazz At Flushing Meadow," *Interiors,* March 1964, p. 107.

39. Lady Malcolm Douglas-Hamilton, unpublished memoirs, Chapter XXIII, p. 160.

40. "Razzmatazz At Flushing Meadow," p. 104.

41. Lady Malcolm Douglas Hamilton, Chapter XXIV, p. 170.

42. "An Architect's Trend-Setting Home For the Fair," *Look,* February 11, 1964, pp. 42–44, and *The Mighty Fair,* p. 17.

43. "Razzmatazz At Flushing Meadow," p. 104.

44. "The House of Good Taste," *Interior Design,* August 1964, p. 89.

45. Peter Lyon, p. 62.

46. Rosemarie Haag Bletter, pp. 92–94.

47. "Razzmatazz At Flushing Meadow," p. 106. *Interior Design* criticized the Formica House's presentation as "deplorable" and considered its style of decoration as "outlandishly outmoded." See "Formica House," *Interior Design,* August 1964, p. 93.

48. *The World's Fair House: American Contemporary Styling At Its Best,* souvenir book, Formica exhibit, 1964, pp. 7, 9, and 15.

49. *The World's Fair House,* pp. 18–19.

50. *The World's Fair House,* pp. 21–22.

51. Walter Dorwin Teague Associates, undated press release, and Peter Lyon, p. 67.

52. Robert Caro, p. 1106.

53. Peter Lyon, pp. 49–50, and American Express, undated press release.

Chapter Five/Harrison

1. For an outline of the philosophical basis of the Fair's program, see Joseph P. Cusker, "The World of Tomorrow: Science, Culture and Community at the New York World's Fair," in Helen A. Harrison, ed., *Dawn of a New Day: The New York World's Fair, 1939/40* (New York: The Queens Museum and New York University Press, 1980), pp. 3–15.

2. *New York World's Fair 1939 Incorporated, Minutes of Executive Committee 1935–36,* p. 71 (August 31, 1936). I am grateful to John Riccardelli for making available to me his bound copies of the minutes of the Executive Committee and the Board of Directors cited hereafter.

3. *Executive Committee Minutes 1935–36,* p. 136.

4. *Information Manual, World's Fair of 1940 in New York.* Entries on "Murals" and "Sculpture," issued April 14, 1940. Courtesy of John Riccardelli.

5. *Information Manual,* Introduction, p. 9.

6. *Executive Committee Minutes 1938,* vol. 1, p. 253 (March 14, 1938).

7. *Board of Directors Minutes 1938,* vol. 1, p. 374 (May 25, 1938).

8. *Official Guide Book, New York World's Fair 1939,* (New York: Exposition Publications, 1939), pp. 89–90.

9. See *Information Manual 1940.*

10. *Executive Committee Minutes 1938,* pp. 108–109 (January 31, 1938); *Board of Directors Minutes 1938,* vol. 1, p. 141 (March 30, 1938). See also *Masterpieces of Art Official Illustrated Catalogue* (New York: Art Associates, Inc., 1939 and 1940 editions).

11. See Helen A. Harrison, "Toward a 'Fit Plastic Language': Six Muralists at the New York World's Fair," in David Shapiro, ed., *Art For the People—New Deal Murals on Long Island* (ex. cat., Hofstra University, Hempstead, N.Y., 1978), pp. 19–25.

12. *Information Manual, New York World's Fair 1939.* Entry on "Murals" (March 7, 1939).

13. "New York World's Fair Commissioned Murals," *Painting and Sculpture in the World of Tomorrow* (Department of Feature Publicity, New York World's Fair 1939), p. 4.

14. Memorandum, Moses to Harrison, July 29, 1960, in New York World's Fair 1964–65 Corporation Records, Box 185, File C3.8 Architectural Embellishment/Production/Construction. These records are on deposit in the Rare Books and Manuscripts Division of the New York Public Library. For the sake of brevity, they will hereafter be cited as NYPL and identified by box and file numbers.

15. Letter, Moses to Harrison, October 28, 1960. NYPL Box 337, File P2.4 Art Committee/Art & Equipment/Participation.

16. Memo, Moses to Clarke, August 11, 1960. NYPL Box 141, File C1.7 Manship, Paul/Sculpture/Construction.

17. Letter, Harrison to Stuart Constable, July 28, 1960. NYPL Box 185, File C3.8 Architectural Embellishment/Production/Construction.

18. Memo, Ames to Constable, (Vice President for Operations), January 11, 1961. NYPL Box 337, File P2.40 Whitney Museum of American Art/Art & Equipment/Participation.

19. Note, Clarke to Moses, March 7, 1961; correspondence, Moses to Harrison, March 14, 1961 and Harrison to Moses, March 22, 1961. NYPL Box 185, File C3.8 Committee on Fountains & Sculpture/Architectural Embellishment/Construction.

20. Letter, Clarke to Moses, May 23, 1961. NYPL Box 185, File C3.8 Architectural Embellishment/Production/Construction.

21. Letter, Clarke to Moses, August 15, 1960. NYPL Box 141, File C1.7 Manship, Paul/Sculpture/Construction. Among the modernists, Noguchi Calder and de Rivera had made works for the earlier fair. Noguchi had executed a "Chassis Fountain" for the garden of the Ford building, while de Rivera had produced two stainless steel reliefs for the pavilion of the Soviet Union. Calder had designed a water-jet fountain for the façade of the Consolidated Edison building.

22. Letter, De Lue to Thomas J. Deegan [Chairman, Executive Committee], November 18, 1959. NYPL Box 141, File C1.7 De Lue, Donald/Sculpture/Construction.

23. Memo, Clarke to Moses, June 26, 1961. NYPL Box 141, File C1.7 Sculpture/Design/Construction.

24. Memo, Committee on Sculpture to Moses, November 24, 1961. NYPL Box 141, File C1.7 Sculpture/Design/Construction. I wish to thank Ardith Mederrick and Ruth Cornish, students at Hofstra University, for their research on the sculpture commissioned by the Fair Corporation.

25. Copies of Roszak's proposal and explanatory sketches are contained in NYPL Box 141.

26. John Canaday, "Art All Over the Fair," *New York Times*, April 25, 1964, p. 12.
27. Letter, De Lue to Moses, April 29, 1964. NYPL Box 141, File C1.7 Sculpture/Design/Construction (1965).
28. Note, Moses to De Lue, May 4, 1964. loc. cit.
29. Telephone interview by the author with Marshall Fredericks, October 10, 1988.
30. Rosenman's association with Moses dated back to the 1920s, when they were both protégés of Governor Al Smith; Rosenman later became Moses's personal attorney. See Robert A. Caro, *The Power Broker: Robert Moses and the Fall of New York* (New York: Alfred A. Knopf, 1974), esp. pp. 720–721. This personal closeness was clearly the deciding factor in disposing Moses toward the idea of a modern art exhibition at Fair expense.
31. Memo, Moses to Constable, December 26, 1961. NYPL Box 141, File C1.7 Gerson, Otto/Sculpture/Construction.
32. Memo, Moses to Constable, June 8, 1962. loc. cit.
33. Note on memo, Constable to Moses, November 21, 1962. loc. cit.
34. Note from Moses on memo, Ames to Constable, September 12, 1961. NYPL Box 337, File P2.40 Barnes Collection/Fine Arts/Participation.
35. Letter, Hirshhorn to Moses, October 26, 1962. NYPL Box 321, File P1.643 Hirshhorn, Joseph (1962–64)/Art Shows/Participation. Plans for the museum are in File P1.643 Hirshhorn, Joseph/Maps.
36. Memo, Moses to Martin Stone, December 23, 1964. loc. cit.
37. Telephone interview by the author with Abram Lerner, Director Emeritus, Hirshhorn Museum and Sculpture Garden, Smithsonian Institution, Washington, D. C., September 25, 1988. According to Lerner, some time after the Fair, Moses proposed installing a portion of Hirshhorn's collection (which had already been accepted by the Smithsonian) in the New York City Building, now the Queens Museum. "I thought it would be a great idea for [the Smithsonian] to have an extension in New York, which they did with the Cooper-Hewitt eventually," Lerner said, but the Smithsonian considered the building unsuitable and vetoed the plan.
38. Letter, Editors and Editorial Board of *Art in America* to Moses, December 26, 1961. NYPL Box 141, File C1.7 Sculpture/Design/Construction.
39. Letter, Goodrich to Selig S. Burrows, [member, Board of Directors], May 31, 1960. NYPL Box 337, File P2.40 Whitney Museum of American Art/Art & Equipment/Participation.
40. NYPL Box 322, File P1.643 Sharp, Evelyn/Art Shows/Participation.
41. NYPL Box 321, File P1.643 Pavilion of Fine Art (1964)/Art Shows/Participation.
42. Letter, Constable to Harris K. Prior [Director, American Federation of Arts], September 15, 1960. NYPL Box 337, File P2.40 American Federation of Arts/Fine Arts/Participation.
43. Memo, Virginia C. Moseley to William E. Potter, November 22, 1963. NYPL Box 321, File P1.643 Pavilion of Fine Art (1964)/Art Shows/Participation.
44. Emily Genauer, "Showplace for Artists: An Old Story Becomes New," New York *Herald Tribune*, August 18, 1963, Sect. 4, p. 1. August Sak's pavilion design is illustrated.
45. John Molleson, "Is Fair Fair About Art?," New York *Herald Tribune*, November 18, 1963, p. 21.
46. Thomas B. Hess, "Moses the Art Slayer Wins Round One," *Art News*, April 1964, p. 25.
47. Telephone interview by the author with Phyllis Braff, former curatorial consultant to the Long Island Arts Center, November 9, 1988. Dr. Braff maintains that it was the financial losses and disillusionment caused by participation in the Fair that led the group to disband shortly thereafter.
48. Walter Carlson, "Pavilion at Fair to Show Fine Art," *New York Times*, May 13, 1964, p. 35.
49. John Canaday, "Art at the Fair: A Lifeless Collection," *New York Times*, June 23, 1964, p. 19.
50. John Canaday, "This Way (and That) to the American Art Shows," *New York Times*, June 28, 1964, Sect. II, p. 13.
51. Charlotte Willard, "In the Art Galleries," *New York Post*, June 27, 1964, p. 46.
52. Emily Genauer, "Finis to Fine Arts," New York *Herald Tribune*, July 17, 1964, p. 8.
53. Braff interview.
54. Ralph Chapman, " 'Mother, Child' Success at Fair," New York *Herald Tribune*, August 31, 1964, p. 12.
55. Dore Ashton, "Three Centuries of American Painting: New York Commentary," *Studio International*, August 1965, p. 89.
56. "Art Hunting in Darkest World's Fair," *Art News*, Summer 1964, p. 36.
57. John Canaday, "Add Fair Art," *New York Times*, June 14, 1964, Sect. II, p. 21.
58. John Canaday, "Pardon The Heresy," *New York Times*, March 29, 1964, Sect. II, p. 19. This was actually done by Midtown Galleries in the American Interiors building, where art competed for attention with furniture, tableware, and hi-fi equipment, and paradoxically in the Hall of Education, where several New York dealers sponsored "Art Gallery '64," a commercial venture that offered works for sale. See "Galleries to Show U. S. Art at the Fair," *New York Times*, April 5, 1964, p. 119.
59. John Canaday, "Art All Over the Fair," *New York Times*, April 25, 1964, p. 12.
60. John Canaday, "Pardon the Heresy."
61. Quoted in Rainer Crone, *Andy Warhol* (New York: Praeger, 1970), p. 30. The "Thirteen Most Wanted Men"—not all of whom were Italian, as Philip Johnson asserted—are illustrated, along with the overpainted mural and Warhol's portrait of Moses, dated 1964 and now unlocated. Warhol recreated the "Most Wanted" series as individual canvases, which were first exhibited in Paris at the Ileana Sonnabend Gallery in 1967. I wish to thank the Gagosian Gallery in New York, which exhibited selections from the series in 1988, for assistance in my research.
62. For a summary of these trends, see Jennifer Wells, "The Sixties: Pop Goes the Market," in *Definitive Statements: American Art 1964–66* (ex. cat., Department of Art, Brown University, Providence, R. I., 1986), pp. 53–61.
63. "Art Hunting in Darkest World's Fair," p. 36. See also Peter Lyon, "A Glorious Nightmare," *Holiday*, July 1964, p. 60.
64. "Hussein Goes to the Fair—And Suddenly It's Chilly," New York *Post*, April 24, 1964, p. 3; Martin Tolchin, "Jordan's Exhibit Assailed by Jews," *New York Times*, April 25, 1964, p. 12.
65. "AJC Questions Fair Ban on Pickets," *Long Island Express*, May 26, 1964, p. 2; Henry Lee, "Fair In Court Fight Over Mural," New York *Daily News*, May 30, 1964, p. 7; John G. Rogers, "That Mural and 'Free Speech,' " New York *Herald Tribune*, July 1, 1964, p. 20; Tania Long, "Fight Breaks Out in Dispute at Fair," *New York Times*, May 1, 1965, p. 63.

Chapter Six/Sheppard

1. George Melrod, "Technology As Theme Park: A Nutshell History of the World's Fairs," *New Observations*, June 1988, p. 4.
2. Peter Lyons, "A Glorious Nightmare," *Holiday*, July 1964, p. 50.
3. Helen A. Harrison, ed., *Dawn of a New Day: The New York World's Fair 1939/40* (New York: The Queens Museum and New York University Press, 1980), p. 1.
4. Bill Davidson, "The Old S.O.B. Does It Again," *Saturday Evening Post*, May 23, 1964, p. 24.
5. Katherine Kuh, "The Day Pop Art Died," *Design in America*, May 23, 1964, p. 24.
6. Vincent J. Scully, Jr., "If This Is Architecture, God Help Us," *Life*, July 31, 1964, p. 9.
7. Katherine Kuh, p. 24.
8. *20th Anniversary, A Disney Retrospective: The New York World's Fair 1964-65* (Walt Disney Productions, 1984), p. 3.
9. *20th Anniversary*, p. 5.
10. George Melrod, p. 7.
11. *20th Anniversary*, p. 5.
12. *Official Guide New York World's Fair 1964/1965* (New York: Time Inc., 1964), p. 145.
13. *Official Guide*, p. 146.
14. *Official Guide*, p. 158.
15. Helen A. Harrison, ed., *Dawn of a New Day*, p. 19.
16. *New York World's Fair Corporation Minutes*, February 14, 1939, p. 299.
17. Thomas Hines, *Populuxe* (New York: Alfred A. Knopf, 1986), p. 66.
18. Andy Warhol and Pat Hackett, *Popism: The Warhol 60s* (New York: Harper and Row, 1980), pp. 64–65.
19. Lyrics by Richard M. Sherman and Robert B. Sherman, © 1963 Wonderland Music Co. Inc.
20. *Pavilion of 2000 Tribes* brochure (Santa Ana: Wycliffe Bible Translators Inc., 1964).
21. E. L. Doctorow, *World's Fair* (New York: Random House, 1985), p. 250.

Applebaum, Stanley, ed. *The New York World's Fair 1939/40.* New York: Dover, 1977.

Ashton, Dore. "Three Centuries of American Painting: New York Commentary." *Studio International,* August 1965, p. 89.

Bright, Randy. *Disneyland: Inside Story.* New York: Harry N. Abrams Inc., 1987.

Caro, Robert A. *The Power Broker: Robert Moses and the Fall of New York.* New York: Alfred A. Knopf, 1974.

Cliff, Ursula. "Fair and Square." *Industrial Design,* March 1961, p. 39.

Crone, Rainer, *Andy Warhol.* New York: Praeger, 1970.

Davidson, Bill, "The Old S.O.B. Does it Again." *Saturday Evening Post,* May 23, 1964, pp. 36–41.

Doctorow, E.L. *World's Fair.* New York: Random House, 1985.

Harrison, Helen A., ed. *Dawn of a New Day: The New York World's Fair, 1939/40.* New York: The Queens Museum and New York University Press, 1980.

Hess, Thomas B. "Moses the Art Slayer Wins Round One." *Art News,* April 1964, p. 25.

Hines, Thomas. *Populuxe.* New York: Alfred A. Knopf, 1986

Hodgson, Godfrey. *America in Our Time.* New York: Doubleday, 1976.

Laurence, William L. *Science at the Fair.* New York: New York World's Fair 1964–1965 Corporation, 1964.

Leuchtenburg, William, E. *A Troubled Feast: American Society Since 1945.* Boston: Little Brown and Company, 1973.

Leuchtenburg, William E. *Franklin D. Roosevelt and the New Deal, 1932–40.* New York: Harper and Row, 1963.

Luckhurst, Kenneth W. *The Story of Exhibitions.* London and New York: Studio Publications, 1951.

Lyon, Peter. "A Glorious Nightmare." *Holiday,* July 1964, pp. 48–67.

Marquis, Alice G. *Hope and Ashes: The Birth of Modern Times 1929–1939.* New York: The Free Press, 1966.

Moses, Robert. *The Fair, The City and The Critics.* Pamphlet. New York: New York World's Fair 1964–1965 Corporation, 1964.

Moses, Robert. *Public Works: A Dangerous Trade.* New York: McGraw-Hill, 1970.

New York World's Fair 1964–1965 Progress Reports. New York: New York World's Fair 1964–1965 Corporation, 1961–1965.

Official Guide Book, New York World's Fair 1939. New York: Exposition Publication, 1939.

Official Guide New York World's Fair 1964/1965. New York: Time Inc., 1964.

O'Neal, William L. *American High: The Years of Confidence, 1945–60.* New York: The Free Press, 1986.

Peary, Danny, ed. *Omni's Screen Flights/Screen Fantasies: The Future According to Science Fiction Cinema.* New York: Doubleday, 1984.

Perry, Ellen; Burns, James T.; and Rowan, Jan. "The Busy Architect's Guide to the World's Fair." *Progressive Architecture,* October 1964, pp. 160–167.

Phillips, Lisa; Hanks, D.A.; Gebhard, D.; Bletter, R.H.; McCoy, E.; Filler, M. *High Styles: Twentieth Century American Design.* Exhibition Catalogue. New York: Whitney Museum of American Art in association with Summit Books, 1985.

Rosen, Laura. ed. *The Liveable City.* Exhibition Catalogue. New York: The Municipal Art Society, 1988.

Rydell, Robert W. *All the World's a Fair: Visions of Empire At American International Expositions, 1876–1916.* Chicago: University of Chicago Press, 1984.

Schickel, Richard. *The Disney Version: The Life, Times, Art and Commerce of Walt Disney.* New York: Simon and Schuster, 1968.

Shapiro, David, ed. *Art for the People— New Deal Murals on Long Island.* Exhibition Catalogue. Hempstead, New York: Hofstra University, 1978.

Swayze, Jay. *Underground Gardens and Homes: The Best of Two Worlds—Above and Below.* Hereford, Texas: Geobuilding Systems, 1980.

Wallock, Leonard, ed. *New York: Culture Capital of the World 1940–1965.* New York: Rizzoli International, 1988.

Warhol, Andy, and Hackett, Pat. *Popism: The Warhol 60s.* New York: Harper and Row, 1980.

Wilson, Richard Guy; Pilgrim, Diane H.; Tashjian, Dickran. *The Machine Age in America 1918–1941.* Exhibition Catalogue. New York: The Brooklyn Museum in association with Harry N. Abrams Inc., 1986.

Zim, Larry; Lerner, Mel; and Rolfes, Herb. *The World of Tomorrow: The 1939 New York World's Fair.* New York: Harper and Row, 1988.